Think of us as a blue plate special with a slice o' pie to boot. Meaty, dependable, and affordable for all. We thought to ourselves: take a big helping of thoughtful guidance and add a side of straightforward instruction and you'd have a start on a pretty good book. Offer it all for less than the price of a couple of movie tickets, and you'd have a great book. In fact, you've got that book in your hands.

Each book in this series of introductory guides isolates one application or topic and aims to get you exploring it quickly and effectively. They're action-based, non-comprehensive, and not filled with a lot of idle chat because our goal is to get users using. Our books are for those who do not accept the premise that if you don't already know, you must be a dummy or an idiot. We believe in using computers to *do* things, not doing things to use computers. Your computer should make your life better, not more complicated. And the truth is, despite the ease of use offered by today's computers, users often need a bridge to help them navigate the digital world. They need a real-world guide and they need it with no nonsense.

You'll be surprised how far you can go in 200 or so pages. Take a look at the Table of Contents to see what we mean. Simple and straightforward—the way using a computer should be. And that's the way each book in this series works. Inside each of these handy books are the essentials of each topic—everything you need to know to get up and running.

Thanks for picking up our books, and drop us a line with your comments.

About the Author

Wallace Wang is the author of over two dozen computer books, including *Microsoft Office For Dummies* and *Steal This Computer Book*. His goal is to teach people that computers may still be way too difficult to use, but with a little bit of knowledge and a healthy skepticism of technology, anyone can learn how to use a computer no matter what their background or previous experience may be. When he's not busy trying to figure out why his computer isn't working, he performs stand-up comedy regularly at the Riviera Comedy Club at the Riviera Hotel and Casino (http://www.theriviera.com) in Las Vegas.

About the Technical Editor

Rowena Portch is a writer, editor, and graphic artist. She has authored more than 50 technical references and 30-plus articles for numerous computer books and magazines. When she's not writing or editing, she enjoys camping with her husband and four children.

Start!

the *no nonsense* guide to

Windows® XP

Wallace Wang

McGraw-Hill/Osborne

New York Chicago San Francisco
Lisbon London Madrid Mexico City
Milan New Delhi San Juan
Seoul Singapore Sydney Toronto

McGraw-Hill/Osborne
2600 Tenth Street
Berkeley, California 94710
U.S.A.

To arrange bulk purchase discounts for sales promotions, premiums, or fund-raisers, please contact **McGraw-Hill**/Osborne at the above address. For information on translations or book distributors outside the U.S.A., please see the International Contact Information page immediately following the index of this book.

Start! The No Nonsense Guide to Windows® XP

1234567890 DOC DOC 0198765433

ISBN 0-07-222739-7

Publisher
Brandon A. Nordin

**Vice President &
Associate Publisher**
Scott Rogers

Acquisitions Editor
Margie McAneny

Senior Project Editor
Carolyn Welch

Acquisitions Coordinator
Tana Allen

Technical Editor
Rowena Portch

Copy Editor
Bob Campbell

Proofreader
Susie Elkind

Indexer
Claire Splan

Computer Designers
Carie Abrew, Dick Schwartz

Illustrators
Michael Mueller, Melinda Moore Lytle,
Lyssa Wald

Series Developers
Greg Simsic, Katy Bodenmiller

Series Interior Design
Greg Simsic, Katy Bodenmiller

Series Cover Design
Greg Simsic, Katy Bodenmiller

This book was composed with Corel VENTURA™ Publisher.

This book is dedicated to all those poor souls out there who still blame themselves for not understanding how computers work. Don't worry, it's not your fault. It's the fault of all the people who make computers so hard to understand in the first place.
—*Wallace Wang*

Thanks to all the wonderful people I've met in the course of pursuing dual careers as a writer and stand-up comedian. Special thanks go out to Margie McAneny and Tana Allen at McGraw-Hill/Osborne along with the technical editor, Rowena, for making sure everything I wrote about actually worked.

All the friendly people at Waterside Productions deserve a big thanks for getting me work all these years, including Bill Gladstone and Matt Wagner. After all these years, I feel like you're part of my family, except that my family doesn't take 15 percent commission off everything I make.

I'd also like to thank all the wonderful people I've worked with over the years, performing in places as fancy as Las Vegas down to total dumps where audience members find it more amusing to fight each other rather than listen to stand-up comedy. Thanks go to Steve Schirripa (who appears in HBO's hit show "The Sopranos") and Don Learned for giving me my break in performing in Las Vegas. Additional thanks go to Kip Addotta, Gerry Bednob, Larry Omaha, Bob Zany, Patrick DeGuire, Bruce Clark, and Dante, who likes grabbing complete strangers in bookstores and showing them his name in my books.

Final thanks go to Cassandra (my wife); Jordan (my son); and Bo, Scraps, Tasha, and Nuit (my cats) for making my life interesting in between changing diapers, cleaning out litter boxes, and wiping up various colored liquids that seem to appear spontaneously on the floor like alien spores from another planet.

Contents

The goal of this book isn't to teach you how to use Windows XP. The goal of this book is to teach you how to make your computer do something useful. In the process of learning to make your computer do something useful, you'll learn how to use Windows XP.

Using Windows XP is like having a (not too bright) butler to help you use your computer. You tell Windows XP what to do and Windows XP translates your commands into instructions that your computer can understand. So the first trick to using Windows XP means knowing what type of commands you can give Windows XP and then choosing the right command so that Windows XP makes your computer do what you want it to do.

The second trick to using Windows XP involves deciphering what your computer may be trying to tell you. Every time you use Windows XP, your computer shows you a list of options you can choose. If you don't understand the options Windows XP shows you, then you won't know what to do next, which is why so many people find computers so intimidating and hard to use.

Besides showing a list of options available to you at all times, Windows XP may also display questions from your computer. When your computer isn't quite sure what you want to do, it asks Windows XP to get more information. Windows XP then displays a question on the screen and waits for you to give it an answer.

Essentially, using Windows XP boils down to three steps:

1. Windows XP displays a list of options and waits for you to choose one of them. This means you have to learn how to interpret the choices Windows XP offers you at any given time.

2. You choose a command that makes the computer do something. This means you have to know how to choose a command with the keyboard or the mouse.

3. Windows XP displays information that shows the results of your last command and then displays more options for you to choose from. This means you have to decipher this additional information that Windows XP shows you.

As long as you remember these three steps, you'll understand the basic idea behind using Windows XP. Now you just have to learn the specific details behind each step, which the rest of this book teaches you.

Keyboard Commands

To use Windows XP, you may need to learn how to give a command through the keyboard. Typically, giving a command through the keyboard involves pressing two or more keys one after another, such as the **CTRL** key followed by the **S** key. To save space and make it easier to read, this book uses a shortcut to tell you when to press two or more keys one after another, such as **ALT+F1**, which means "Press the **ALT** key and then press the **F1** key, then let both of them go."

Sometimes you may need to press and hold down three keys one after another, such as **CTRL+ALT+DELETE**, which means "Press the **CTRL** key, followed by the **ALT** key and then the **DELETE** key, then let go of all three keys." Most keyboard commands involve pressing one or two keys, but a few may require you to press three keys one after another.

Mouse Commands

Many times, you'll need to give a command to Windows XP using the mouse. Generally, there are four ways you can use your mouse to give a command:

- **Point**   This means you use the mouse to move the mouse pointer over an item on the screen.
- **Click**   This means you press the left mouse button once and then let go.
- **Double-click**   This means you press the left mouse button twice in rapid succession.
- **Right-click**   This means that you press the right mouse button once and then let go.

How This Book Is Organized

This book consists of seven chapters that explain how to use different parts of Windows XP.

- Chapter 1: Acquaint   This chapter explains how to give commands through the keyboard and the mouse, and how to interpret the information that Windows XP displays on the screen.

- Chapter 2: Customize Windows XP   This chapter explains how to customize Windows XP so that you can change its colors, appearance, or behavior.

- Chapter 3: Organize Your Data   This chapter explains how to save and organize your data on your computer.

- Chapter 4: Connect   This chapter explains how to use the Internet and e-mail using Windows XP.

- Chapter 5: Working with Windows XP   This chapter explains how to install, run, and remove programs from your computer.

- Chapter 6: Have Fun   This chapter explains how to play music, watch and record movies, and store digital pictures on your computer.

- Chapter 7: Enhance Windows XP   This chapter explains how to improve Windows XP through updates and software patches, or additional tools that Microsoft developed but didn't have time to include in Windows XP.

You can just read the chapters you want and skip over the others, or you can read the book straight through from start to finish. In any case, the first five chapters contain the most important information about using Windows, while the last two chapters contain optional information that isn't entirely necessary to know when using Windows XP.

Finally, there are two appendices, which cover Windows XP shortcuts and some popular web sites you might want to explore.

Acquaint

In technical terms, Windows XP is a special program known as an "operating system." In plain English, that means your computer speaks one language but you speak another, so Windows XP acts as a translator between you and your computer. When you give a command to Windows XP, Windows XP translates that command to make the computer do something such as open a word processor or play a game. Then your computer tells Windows XP to display information on the screen to ask what else you want the computer to do.

Basically when you use any computer, you engage in this type of back and forth conversation. The computer gives you options on what you can do, you give the computer a command, and the computer obeys and then gives you new options on what you can do next. The operating system that your computer uses simply acts as the middleman that passes your commands on to the computer and displays any information from the computer back for you to look at.

To control any computer that runs Windows XP, you need to learn two things: how to give commands to Windows XP and how to decipher the information that Windows XP displays back to you.

Interact

You give commands to your computer with a keyboard or mouse. Some computers have a trackball or touch pad in place of a mouse, but they work just like a mouse with slight variations. Ideally, you could point to items on your computer screen to show your computer what you want it to do, but since computers can't see your finger, you have to use the mouse as a pointing device instead. When you point the mouse at something on your screen and click the left mouse button, you tell your computer, "See that command that I'm pointing at? That's the command I want you to follow."

Pointing is a fast and easy way to control your computer, but sometimes your computer needs specific information such as a phone number that you want to dial or a web site address that you want to visit. Since your computer isn't likely to display this type of information on the screen for you to point at, you have to type this information using the keyboard. So when your computer asks a question such as "How many pages do you want me to print?" you can answer by typing a number.

The Mouse

The *mouse pointer* appears as a little arrow on your computer screen. When you slide the mouse around with your hand, you move the mouse pointer around on your computer screen.

> **AS A MATTER OF FACT** *The mouse pointer often changes its appearance to give you information. For example, if your computer is busy doing something, the mouse pointer may turn into an hourglass. If you move the mouse over a web page and the mouse pointer turns into a hand, that means you just moved the mouse over a link to another web page.*

Choose Commands

At any given time, your computer displays commands on the screen for you to choose. These commands commonly appear as menu items, buttons, or icons. To choose a command, you simply move the mouse pointer over the command you want and then click the left mouse button once (see Figure 1-1).

To see how you can control your computer with the mouse, move the mouse pointer directly over the green Start button at the bottom-left corner of the screen and click the left mouse button (left-click). When you click the Start button, the **Start** menu pops up.

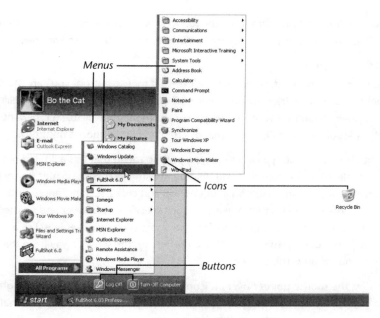

Figure 1-1 *The different ways Windows XP displays commands.*

Slide the mouse pointer over the **All Programs** command. You can either click the **All Programs** command or wait a few seconds, without clicking the mouse button at all, and another menu pops up, listing the names of all the programs stored on your computer. You may notice that some program names on this menu display a little arrow pointing to the right. This right-pointing arrow tells you, "Hey, if you move or click the mouse pointer over me, you can see yet another menu that's full of additional commands related to that particular program."

> **AS A MATTER OF FACT** *Sometimes Windows XP lets you see an additional menu or information if you just move the mouse pointer over an item on the screen and wait a second or two. To see how this works, move the mouse pointer over the clock in the lower-right corner of your screen. After the mouse pointer stays over the clock for a moment, a little window appears that tells you the day and date.*

Move the mouse pointer over **Accessories** near the top of the program list. If you click **Accessories**, or simply move the mouse pointer over it, another menu pops up. Slide the mouse pointer down to WordPad, which appears at the bottom of the list, and click the left mouse button. The WordPad window pops up, ready for you to type something. What you just did was navigate through the **Start** menu and use the left mouse button to tell Windows XP that you wanted to run the WordPad program.

To close the WordPad program, click the red icon with an X in it. This icon, known as the *Close box,* appears in the upper-right corner of the WordPad window.

Display Commands

Besides the click command, where you click the left mouse button, you can also click the right mouse button (right-click). When you click the right button, you're telling your computer, "Don't show me all the possible commands available. I just want to see a short list of the most likely commands I might want to choose right now."

The right-click command typically displays a pop-up menu that lists a limited range of options related to the item that you pointed at with the mouse pointer. To try this out, move the mouse anywhere on your desktop and click the right mouse button. A little pop-up menu appears that displays options specific to whatever you pointed at on the desktop. To make this pop-up menu go away, you can either left-click a command in the pop-up menu, left-click anywhere on the screen away from the pop-up menu, or press the Esc key.

Now move the mouse pointer over an icon on your desktop and click your right mouse button. Notice that this pop-up menu displays different commands that are specific to what you point at with the mouse pointer.

Figure 1-2
The right-click command displays a pop-up menu.

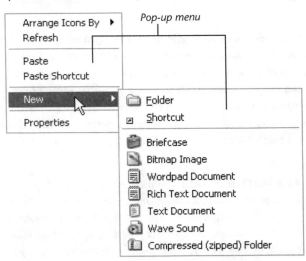

AS A MATTER OF FACT *The pop-up menu lists different commands, depending on which item you have selected when you use the right-click command.*

Select Data

Just as you can use the mouse to point to different commands, you can also use the mouse to select any data that you want to modify, such as text in a word processor or pictures in a graphics program. To select such items, you can't just point and click on them as you do with a menu command or icon. Instead, you have to select data by highlighting it with the mouse.

To highlight data on your computer screen, you first have to move the mouse pointer to the beginning of the data that you want to select. Next, you have to press down the left mouse button and drag the mouse pointer over the data you want to select. When you're done selecting data, you let go of the left mouse button and Windows XP highlights your selected data.

When you select graphics, Windows XP shows a rectangle made up of dotted lines to show you how much you've selected with the mouse so far. As you move the mouse, this dotted-line rectangle grows or shrinks until you release the left mouse button to stop selecting items.

Once you've selected data, you can then choose a command to modify that data. In case you suddenly decide you don't want to highlight the data you just selected, left-click anywhere on the screen away from the data you've selected. Once you click away from the data, Windows XP no longer highlights your selected data.

Scroll

Your mouse may have a little rubber wheel that you can spin around or press with your thumb or fingertip. This middle button, called a mouse wheel, lets you scroll data on your screen up or down.

AS A MATTER OF FACT *The mouse wheel is handy for reading large word processor documents or web pages that don't fit completely on your computer screen. Some programs do not support the mouse wheel, so it's possible that you will press or scroll the mouse wheel and nothing will happen.*

To use the mouse wheel, simply move the mouse pointer over the text that you want to scroll and then spin the wheel up or down. When you spin the wheel up, the text scrolls up. When you spin the wheel down, the text scrolls down.

If you push the mouse wheel down once, the mouse pointer turns into a special scroll icon that shows black up and down arrows. When the scroll icon appears, that means you can make text scroll up or down just by moving the mouse up or down. The farther up you move the mouse pointer, the faster your text scrolls up, and the farther down you move it, the faster the text scrolls down. The closer you move the mouse pointer toward the scroll icon in the middle of the screen, the slower your text scrolls either up or down. To return to regular scroll mode, click the wheel button again.

The Keyboard

Normally you use the keyboard to type letters, numbers, or symbols, but you can also use the keyboard to give commands to your computer.

> **AS A MATTER OF FACT** *Sometimes choosing a command from the keyboard immediately tells the computer to follow a command, but sometimes it's just a shortcut to display a menu faster than when using the mouse to display that same menu.*

One-Key Commands

Many keyboards display a special Windows logo key and a Menu key (see Figure 1-3). The Windows logo key acts as a shortcut for clicking the Start button with the mouse. Press the Windows logo key (if your keyboard has one) and the **Start** menu magically appears. (Isn't this faster than fumbling with the mouse, moving the mouse pointer over the Start button, and then clicking the left mouse button?)

The Menu key acts as a shortcut for the mouse right-click command. Select an item, then press the Menu key to view a shortcut menu for that item.

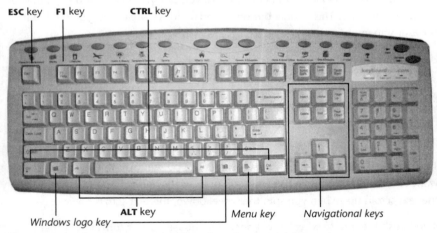

ESC key   **F1** key   **CTRL** key

Windows logo key ———   **ALT** key   Menu key   Navigational keys

Figure 1-3 *Common command keys found on most keyboards.*

Every keyboard has an **F1** function key. When you press the **F1** function key, a help window appears for the program that you're currently using. (You'll learn more about getting help later in this chapter. In case you pressed the **F1** function key and a help window popped up, you can get rid of it by clicking in the Close box, that big red box in the upper right-hand corner with an X in it, of the help window.)

Perhaps the most useful key to remember on your keyboard is the Escape (**ESC**) key. When you press the **ESC** key, you're telling Windows XP, "Get rid of any menus on my screen." To see how the **ESC** key works, press the Windows logo key so the **Start** menu pops up and clutters your screen. Now press the **ESC** key and magically the entire **Start** menu disappears.

Two-Key Commands

It would be nice if your keyboard had different keys to make your computer do everything you could possibly think of doing. Unfortunately, such a keyboard would have to contain dozens of separate keys. So instead of building unwieldy keyboards, computer manufacturers added special modifier keys on keyboards. The two modifier keys that every keyboard includes are the Control (**CTRL**) key and the Alternate (**ALT**) key.

If you press the **CTRL** key by itself, nothing happens. Go ahead and try it to satisfy your curiosity. You always hold down the **CTRL** key before you press another key, such as a letter like the **s** key. When this book tells you to hold down the **CTRL** key and then press another key to give a command, you'll see something like this: **CTRL+S**. This just means that you have to hold down the **CTRL** key, then press the **s** key, and then let go of both keys.

If your keyboard doesn't have a Windows logo key, you can still open the **Start** menu from the keyboard if you press **CTRL+ESC**.

> **AS A MATTER OF FACT**   *Many programs use the same two-key commands for common tasks such as Save (**CTRL+S**) and Print (**CTRL+P**).*

The **ALT** key works the same way as the **CTRL** key. In many programs, you can give a command if you hold down the **ALT** key and then press another key such as the **F1** key (**ALT+F1**).

The **ALT** key also lets you choose pull-down menus within a program to view menu commands without using the mouse. To see how this works, press the Windows logo key to display the **Start** menu. Move the mouse pointer over **All Programs** and wait a few seconds. A pop-up menu appears. Move the mouse pointer over **Accessories** and when another menu pops up, click **Paint**. The Microsoft Paint program appears.

Now press the **ALT** key. Windows XP highlights the **File** menu in the upper left-hand corner. Press the **UP ARROW** or **DOWN ARROW** key and the pull-down menu appears. Press the **LEFT ARROW** or **RIGHT ARROW** key and you can view the command stored in a different pull-down menu. Press **ESC** and the menu disappears from view.

> **AS A MATTER OF FACT** *Anything you can do with the mouse you can also do with the keyboard. You can actually use the keyboard just like a mouse to point and choose commands. This can come in handy in case your mouse ever breaks. Once you get more experienced and comfortable with your computer, you may find that it's faster to use the keyboard to choose a command rather than point to that same command using the mouse.*

To get rid of the Paint program, you could click the Close box in the Paint window, but to see how to close a program with the keyboard, just press **ALT+F4**. The Paint program window disappears.

Navigational Commands

In addition to the mouse pointer, many programs such as word processors and spreadsheets display a *cursor,* which usually appears as a blinking vertical line. The cursor lets you point without using the mouse. Wherever the cursor appears, that's where any text you type will appear next.

To move the cursor around, you have to use your keyboard's navigational keys. The four common navigational keys are the arrow keys, also called the cursor keys, which point in four different directions: up, down, right, and left. When you press one of the arrow keys, you move the cursor in that direction (up, down, right, or left).

Since moving the cursor one character or line at a time with the arrow keys can be tedious, computer keyboards also include additional navigational keys with labels such as **HOME**, **END**, **PAGE UP** (**PGUP**), or **PAGE DOWN** (**PGDN**). These keys don't always work the same within different programs, but in most word processors when you press the **HOME** key, you move the cursor to the beginning of a line. When you press the **END** key, you move the cursor to the end of a line. When you press **PGUP** or **PGDN**, you scroll text on the screen one page up or down.

> **AS A MATTER OF FACT** *You can also use the **CTRL** and **ALT** modifier keys with the navigational keys. In some programs, pressing the **CTRL** and **RIGHT ARROW** keys (**CTRL+RIGHT ARROW**) moves the cursor right to the beginning of the next word. Likewise, pressing **CTRL+LEFT ARROW** moves the cursor left to the beginning of the current or preceding word.*

View

Depending on what you're doing with your computer, Windows XP displays information on the screen in three ways: on the desktop, in a window, or in a dialog box.

When Windows XP is waiting for you to give it a command, it displays the desktop. Once you start one or more programs, your programs appear in one or more windows. When you choose a command and the computer needs more information before carrying out your command, a dialog box appears. Through the combination of the desktop, windows, and dialog boxes, Windows XP gives you information and accepts your commands to control your computer.

The Desktop

The *desktop* is the first screen that Windows XP displays after you turn on your computer. Whenever you see the desktop, that means Windows XP is asking you, "Okay, I'm ready. What do you want me to do now?"

AS A MATTER OF FACT *The desktop always remains on your screen even when you play a game or connect to the Internet, although it may be hidden from view when you run one or more programs.*

Like the top of an office desk that may hold a telephone, a pad of paper, a calendar, and a calculator for you to use, the Windows XP desktop also provides a space to store the tools you need to do your work. The main space of the Windows XP desktop, called the *background* or *wallpaper,* covers the entire screen and can display colors, patterns, or pictures to decorate your computer screen.

Two of the tools that appear on top of the background are *icons* and the *taskbar.* Icons are little pictures that represent a specific program or file stored on your computer. Icons act like the speed-dial feature of a telephone. Just as the speed-dial feature lets you call a telephone number without typing in the complete phone number, icons let you start a program without having to open up the **Start** menu and scroll through a long list until you find the program or file you want.

While icons offer a shortcut to start your programs, the taskbar provides the tools you need to run, copy, move, rename, or delete every program or file stored on your computer. Any time you want to make your computer do something, you can always tell it what to do through the taskbar. The most prominent feature of the taskbar is the Start button (see Figure 1-4).

Figure 1-4
*What's on the
Windows XP
desktop.*

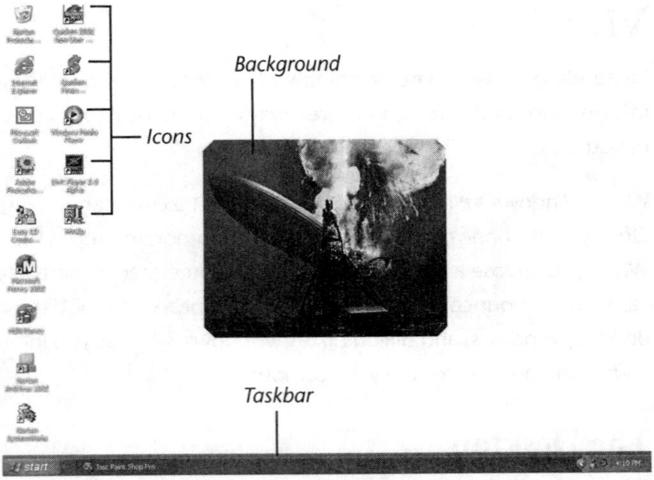

Background

Icons

Taskbar

start

Windows

When you start a program or switch to a currently running program, Windows XP displays your program in a *window* that appears as a rectangle covering part or most of the screen. If you have several programs running at the same time, each program appears in a separate window; for instance, one window may run a game and a second window may run an Internet browser (see Figure 1-5). If you open several files using the same program, such as a word processor, each file appears in a separate window as well.

The content of every window depends on the type of program running; for instance, a spreadsheet program will have different content from a graphics program. The top of every window always displays a thick upper border known as the *title bar*. The title bar lists the name of the program inside the window and sometimes lists the name of the file displayed in that window. The left-most icon is called the *control box*. If you click the control box, a menu appears, listing commands that allow you to resize or move the window.

The three boxes in the far-right side of the title bar are called the Minimize button, the Maximize button, and the Close box. To see how these buttons work, press the Windows logo key so that the **Start** menu appears. Click **All Programs**. When a list of programs appears, click **Accessories** and then click **Notepad**. The Notepad window appears.

Click the Minimize button. Suddenly the Notepad window shrinks and appears as a tiny box on the taskbar. Click the Notepad button on the taskbar and the Notepad window magically springs to life again.

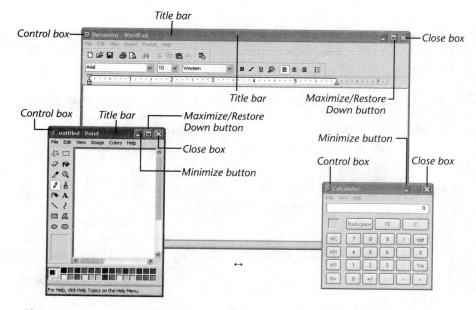

Control box — Title bar — Close box

Title bar — Maximize/Restore Down button

Control box — Title bar — Maximize/Restore Down button — Minimize button

Close box — Minimize button

Control box — Close box

Figure 1-5 *Windows XP displays each program or file in a separate window.*

Now click the Maximize button in the Notepad window. Suddenly the Notepad grows in size and fills up the entire screen. Notice, too, how the Maximize button has changed in appearance. When it resembles two stacked windows, it is called the Restore button. Click the Restore button to restore the window to its original size. Suddenly your Notepad window shrinks back down to covering part of the screen instead of gobbling the whole screen. Click the Close box of the Notepad window to close the Notepad program.

Dialog Boxes

A *dialog box* covers part of the screen and appears only after you choose a command and the computer needs more specific information, such as how many pages to print or where you want to save a file. When a dialog box appears, it won't go away until you answer the question that the dialog box is asking or click the Cancel button (see Figure 1-6). You can also press **ESC** to make the dialog box go away.

The simplest dialog box asks a question or displays information and waits for you to either acknowledge the message or give further instruction. *Buttons* are the main way to tell the dialog box what you want the computer to do next. For example, OK means that you acknowledge the message, and Cancel means you do not want to perform the action.

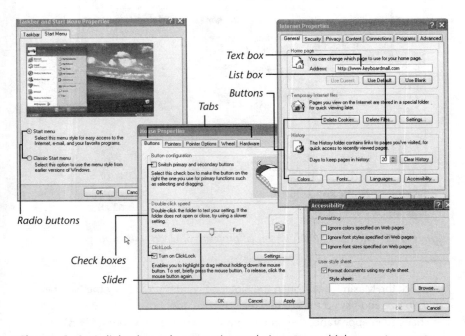

Figure 1-6   *A dialog box asks a question and gives you multiple ways to answer.*

Sometimes a dialog box may offer several options organized in a list as *check boxes* or *radio buttons.* Check boxes let you choose one or more options. Radio buttons let you choose one option out of several.

If a dialog box needs to offer you a long list of options, it may display your choices in a *list box* instead. A list box lets you choose one option out of many from a list that pops up.

When a dialog box needs to give you a choice of a limited range of numbers, it may display your choices as a *slider.* By moving the slider, you can choose the number that you want to use.

Sometimes a dialog box will simply display a *text box* so that you can type in an answer, such as typing in the name of a file. If a dialog box needs to display a large number of choices, it may organize them on separate *tabs.* By clicking on each tab, you can see related options you can choose.

To see what a real-life dialog box looks like, click the Start button or press the Windows logo key. Click **Control Panel**. When the Control Panel window appears, click Appearance And Themes.

From within the Appearance And Themes window, click Change The Desktop Background. A Display Properties dialog box appears. To get rid of the dialog box without making any changes, click the Cancel button or press **ESC** to make the dialog box disappear. When you click the OK button, you're telling Windows XP, "Did you see all the information I gave you in that dialog box? Well, use those changes to follow my commands and then make the dialog box go away."

Get Help

When you run into problems using Windows XP, you can always ask Windows XP for help. Unfortunately, Windows XP doesn't understand English (or Spanish, or French, or any other language that most humans understand), so when you ask for help, Windows XP displays a list of possible topics that it thinks you might want help on, such as printing, connecting your computer to a network, or playing music. You have to choose a topic that you think may contain an answer to your question.

After you choose a topic, Windows XP asks you, "Here's another list of more detailed topics for you to choose from. Which one do you think will answer your question?" After you choose yet another topic, you may have to repeat this process one or more times before Windows XP finally offers a list of detailed instructions or tasks that can solve a specific problem.

Although the help that Windows XP provides isn't perfect, it may still help you out if you can't get your question answered by a real live person sitting next to you.

The Help Window

To get help from Windows XP, you have to open the Windows XP help window. To do this, click the Start button and then click **Help and Support**. Once the Windows XP help window opens, you can ask for help by clicking the choices that Windows XP offers or by typing a word or phrase about the subject you want help on.

Click

When the Windows XP help window appears, it lists different help topics, but unless you know what type of help each topic offers, you won't know which

topic to choose. Basically, Windows XP offers two types of help: general
information about using Windows XP and troubleshooting suggestions when
things don't work.

*AS A MATTER OF FACT Windows XP stores some of the same general
information and troubleshooting advice under different help topics. For example,
you can find the same troubleshooting advice for installing a joystick on your
computer by looking in the "Music, video, games, and photos" help topic, the
"Hardware" help topic, or the "Fixing a problem" help topic.*

Think of the help window as a book that you can scroll through, page by page.
As you click your way through the help window, you may want to go back to a
previous page that you already viewed. When this happens, you can click the
Back button. If you already clicked the Back button and suddenly decide you want
to go forward to the page that you just saw, click the Forward button. If you're
completely lost within the help window and just want to start all over again, click
the Home button to display the first page of the help window.

To see how to get help through your mouse, click the Start button to display the **Start**
menu. Then click **Help and Support** to display the Help window.

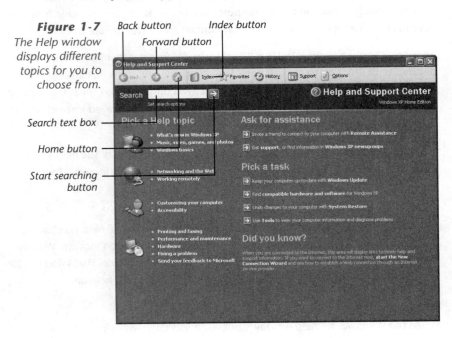

Figure 1-7
*The Help window
displays different
topics for you to
choose from.*

Back button   Index button

Forward button

Search text box

Home button

Start searching
button

Click the Windows Basics help topic. The Help window displays a list of topics related to using Windows XP. Click Core Windows tasks. A new list of topics appears. Click Working With Programs.

Windows XP displays a list of tasks related to running and using programs. Click Quit A Program. The Help window lists step-by-step instructions to show you how to quit a program.

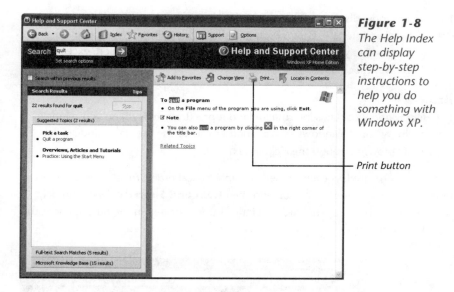

Figure 1-8
The Help Index can display step-by-step instructions to help you do something with Windows XP.

— *Print button*

Once you find the information you're looking for, you can click the Print button and print a hard copy of these instructions.

Search

Clicking your way through the Help window can be tiresome and tedious, so you may want to take matters in your own hands and just type a specific word or phrase that you want to search for help on. To do this, you need to type in the Search box.

The Search box lets you tell Windows XP, "I need help on this topic, so give me a list of all help topics that you think might help me." Since Windows XP doesn't understand complete sentences, you can just type one or two words in the Search box instead. So rather than type "I need help playing a CD in my computer," you can just type one or two words to identify your problem, such as "play CD." When you condense an entire question into one or two words, those words are called *keywords*.

When you type a keyword in the Search box, Windows XP digs through its long list of help topics and displays only those help topics that contain your keywords. At this point, you need to click the help topic that you think will give you the help you need.

To see how much faster the Search box can be, click the Start button to display the **Start** menu. Then click **Help and Support** to display the Help window. Click in the Search box, type **quit**, and press **ENTER** or click the Start Searching button. (It doesn't matter if you type in lowercase, uppercase, or a mixture of both.)

The Help window displays a list of tasks related to your keyword. In this case, it only displays a single task, Quit A Program. Click Quit A Program and you'll see the exact same help you saw using the mouse in the preceding section, except the Search box was much faster.

Browse

The Help window contains information about practically everything you might want to know about Windows XP. For another way to use the Help window, you can simply browse through the Help Index.

The Help Index displays every subject, in alphabetical order. To see how the Help Index works, click the Start button and then **Help and Support**. Once the Help And Support window opens, click the Index button located in the button bar at the top of the window.

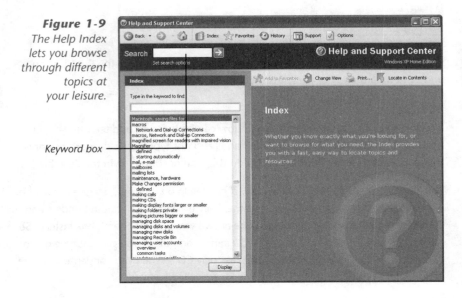

Figure 1-9
The Help Index lets you browse through different topics at your leisure.

Keyword box

Click in the Keyword box and type an **M**. The Help Index immediately displays all subjects starting with *M*, such as macros, magnifier, and mail. Type an **o** and you'll notice that subjects beginning with *MO* appear in the Help Index.

> ***AS A MATTER OF FACT*** *You can always press the* **PGDN** *or* **PGUP** *keys, or use the scroll wheel of your mouse, to scroll up or down in the Help Index list.*

Add an **N** to the end of the letters you have typed into the index box to display the Monitors help topic, click Automatic Turnoff, and then click the Display button. The Help Index displays instructions for turning off your monitor automatically. Click the Close box of the Help window to make it go away.

Turn Off

To use a typical electrical appliance, such as a hair dryer, a television set, or a lamp, you turn it on and off using the same switch. But while you can turn a computer on using the on switch, don't press that same switch to turn off your computer! If you suddenly turn the power off on your computer, there's a chance that Windows XP will damage or even completely lose any data stored on your hard disk.

So when you want to turn off your computer, let Windows XP turn off your computer instead. That way, Windows XP has one last chance to save all your data before turning off your computer. To turn off your computer, click the Start button and click **Turn Off Computer**. A dialog box displays three buttons: Stand By, Turn Off, Restart. Click Turn Off and Windows XP obediently carries out your command.

The Stand By button leaves your computer on but reduces power to conserve electricity, which can be especially useful for laptop computers. To revive a computer that had been put on Stand By, you may have to tap a key, move the mouse, or press the On switch.

The Restart button simply shuts down and starts your computer up again, which can be handy in case your computer starts acting strangely, for instance, if the mouse moves erratically or the keyboard doesn't work. Often, restarting your computer (also called *rebooting*) can fix any minor glitches with your computer.

2

Customize Windows XP

Although Windows XP works exactly the same on every computer, it doesn't necessarily have to look the same. Just as Ford or Honda sells several million cars that work exactly alike, they also give customers a chance to customize their particular car with the features, colors, and accessories that they want.

Likewise, you can also customize the appearance and behavior of your particular copy of Windows XP. Any changes you make are completely optional, but they can make Windows XP look nicer or just work in a way that's more comfortable for you.

For example, you might find that staring at the same screen all day might get boring, so Windows XP lets you spice things up by adding your own pictures. Now, every time you start up Windows XP, you can see a picture of your family, your dog, or your favorite scenery ready to greet you before you begin to work.

Besides making Windows XP more decorative, you can also make it more functional, too. Most people tend to use a handful of programs, so for a quick way to load your favorite programs in a hurry, Windows XP lets you create icons to represent your programs. Just one click on these icons can load your programs right away so you can do something useful or just have fun with your computer.

The Desktop

You can change the appearance of anything you see on the screen. The most obvious part of Windows XP that you might want to change is the desktop, which appears every time you turn on your computer. Most people change the desktop just to make their computer look pretty, but there are also ways to change the desktop to make Windows XP easier for you to use.

Open the Display Properties Dialog Box

To customize most features of Windows XP, you have to go through the Display Properties dialog box, which you can open through the desktop or through the Start button.

To open the Display Properties dialog box from the desktop, right-click on any blank area on the desktop. When a pop-up menu appears, click **Properties** to see the Display Properties dialog box. You may need to click on a tab, such as Settings or Appearance, to make certain changes.

Figure 2-1

The Display Properties dialog box provides options to customize Windows XP.

AS A MATTER OF FACT *In case you can't see the desktop because you have already loaded one or more programs, right-click the taskbar and, when a menu pops up, click **Show the Desktop**.*

You can also open the Display Properties dialog box if you click the Start button, click **Control Panel**, and click Appearance and Themes. Then click the particular task you want to do, such as Change the desktop background or Choose a screensaver. This opens the Display Properties dialog box.

> **AS A MATTER OF FACT** *If you click Apply in the Display Properties dialog box, you can see what your settings will look like on your screen without removing the Display Properties dialog box. If you're happy with your changes, click OK to use your settings and remove the dialog box. Otherwise, click Cancel and choose different settings.*

So throughout this chapter when you read instructions that tell you to open the Display Properties dialog box, refer back to this section in case you forget the specific procedures to see the Display Properties dialog box.

The Background

The background, or wallpaper, dominates your computer screen every time you turn on your computer, so it's only natural that most people want to change the background first. You can change the background to display a solid color such as red or light purple, or a picture that you scanned or captured with a digital camera.

> **AS A MATTER OF FACT** *Remember that you, and anyone else with a view of your monitor, may see your background every time you turn on your computer, so choose a background that you won't mind seeing over and over again.*

Colors

You can change your background to a solid color from a list of colors or through custom color that you can create on your own. To see how to change the color of your background, open the Display Properties dialog box and click the Desktop tab.

Click in the Background list box and click None (see Figure 2-2). Then click the Color list box. A palette of different colors appears. At this point, you can click on one of these colors or, if you want even more variety, click the Other button.

If you click the Other button, a Color dialog box appears that displays a range of different colors. Click on a color and click OK. The Display Properties dialog box appears again, showing you what your chosen color looks like in the drawing of the monitor in the top of the dialog box. Click OK if you're happy with the color you chose.

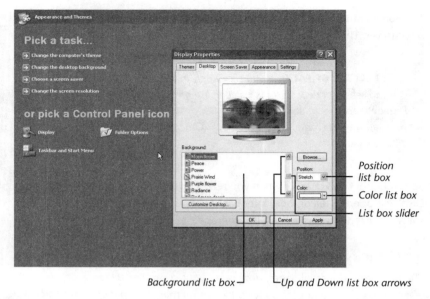

Position list box

Color list box

List box slider

Background list box ┘   └─Up and Down list box arrows

Figure 2-2   *The Background list box shows all the built-in themes you can use for your background.*

Pictures

You can also change your background to display one of many pictures that comes with Windows XP. To change the background to one of these pictures, open the Display Properties dialog box and click the Desktop tab. The Background box lists all the different background images that come with Windows XP, such as Tulips or Crystal. To scroll through this list, you can either press the **UP ARROW** or **DOWN ARROW** key, press the **PGUP** or **PGDN** key, click the Up or Down arrow in the Background list box, or move the mouse pointer over the list box slider and drag the mouse up or down.

Each time you click or highlight a theme, the monitor in the Display Properties dialog box shows you what your choice looks like. When you're happy with a particular theme, click OK.

Custom Pictures

Despite all the choices that Windows XP gives you, you might not like any of the pictures available for your background. As an alternative, you can choose any graphic image stored in a bitmap (.bmp), JPEG (.jpg), or GIF (.gif) file format. Microsoft Paint, the paint program that comes with Windows XP, can create .bmp files. If you want to create .jpg or .gif files, you need to use a separate program.

To change your background to a picture that you have stored on your hard disk, open the Display Properties dialog box and click the Desktop tab. The Background box lists all the graphic images that come with Windows XP and that you've stored in your My Pictures folder. If the graphic file you want to use does not appear in the Background list box, click the Browse button.

A Browse dialog box appears. Click the graphic file you want to use. If you can't find the file you want, you may need to click a folder and click the Open button, click in the Up One Level button, or click in the Look In list box to look for the file on a different disk.

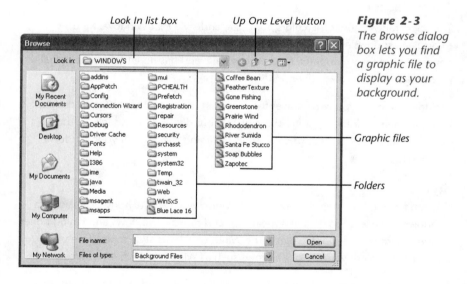

Look In list box   *Up One Level button*

Figure 2-3
The Browse dialog box lets you find a graphic file to display as your background.

Graphic files

Folders

When you find the file you want to use, click that filename and then click the Open button. The Display Properties dialog box shows you what your image looks like in the monitor in the top of the dialog box.

For more options to display your picture as a background, click in the Position list box and choose either Center, Tile, or Stretch. Center displays your chosen graphic image in the middle of the screen. Tile displays your chosen graphic image multiple times in rows and columns until it fills the entire screen. Stretch displays a single picture of your graphic image but stretches that one image to fill the entire screen.

Click Apply to see how your chosen image appears on the screen. When you're happy with the way your chosen graphic image looks, click OK.

Figure 2-4 *How the same graphic image appears when centered, tiled, or stretched.*

Appearance

The appearance defines the colors, font size, and style that Windows XP uses to display windows and dialog boxes on your screen. Like the background, the appearance of your computer is purely cosmetic and has no effect on the actual performance of Windows XP.

Windows XP gives you two choices for changing the appearance of your desktop: by using themes or by changing the parts of your desktop individually. A theme changes multiple settings at once, such as changing the color of your windows and desktop.

Style

You can choose from two different styles: Windows XP and Windows Classic. The Windows XP style is the default appearance and displays windows and dialog boxes in bright, almost cartoonish, colors. The Windows Classic style more closely resembles the older versions of Windows such as Windows 2000 or Windows 98.

To switch styles, open the Display Properties dialog box and click the Appearance tab. Now click in the Windows And Buttons list box and choose either Windows XP style or Windows Classic style. Your chosen style appears in windows and dialog boxes in the top of the Display Properties dialog box. Click OK when you're happy with your chosen style.

Colors

Besides changing the style that Windows XP uses to display windows and dialog boxes, you can also change the colors that appear in a window or dialog box as well. To change colors, open the Display Properties dialog box and click the Appearance tab.

Now click in the Colors list box and choose either Default (blue), Olive Green, or Silver. Your chosen colors appear in the sample windows and dialog boxes at the top of the Display Properties dialog box. Click OK when you're happy with your chosen colors.

Fonts

You can also change the font size that Windows XP uses in windows and dialog boxes. That way, you can make them larger and easier to read. To change fonts, open the Display Properties dialog box and click the Appearance tab. Now click in the Font list box and choose either Normal, Large Fonts, or Extra Large Fonts. Your chosen fonts appear in the sample windows and dialog boxes at the top of the Display Properties dialog box. Click OK when you're happy with your chosen fonts.

Themes

If you want a fast way to change the appearance of your desktop, use a theme. A *theme* provides a consistent look for Windows XP. If you'd rather have more control over the appearance of individual parts of your desktop, don't use a theme.

To choose a theme, open the Display Properties dialog box and click the Themes tab. Then click the Themes list box and choose a theme, such as Windows Classic or Windows XP. Your chosen theme appears in the sample box in the bottom of the Display Properties dialog box. Click OK when you're happy with your chosen theme.

Resolution

In technical terms, the screen resolution determines the number of pixels that your computer uses to display images on your screen in both vertical and horizontal directions such as 800 × 600 (800 pixels vertically and 600 pixels horizontally). In nontechnical terms, a pixel is just a dot on your screen, so the more pixels your computer uses to display an image, the sharper that image appears on your screen.

The good part about choosing the highest resolution possible is that your computer displays crisp, sharp images on your screen. The bad part is that the higher the resolution, the smaller everything looks on your screen. It's possible to choose such a high resolution that everything on your screen looks too tiny to look at.

To change the resolution of your computer, open the Display Properties dialog box and click the Settings tab. Click to the right or left of the Screen resolution slider, or move the mouse pointer over the slider and drag the mouse left or right. As the slider moves, the dialog box displays your chosen screen resolution underneath (see Figure 2-5).

Click in the Color quality list box and choose a color quality. Generally, it's best to choose the highest color quality available. Now click OK when you're happy with your chosen screen resolution.

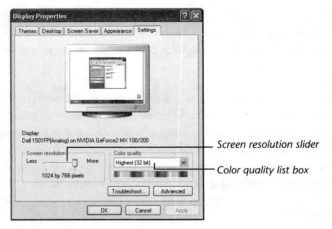

Figure 2-5
You can change the screen resolution and color quality to make images on your screen sharper and easier to read.

Screen resolution slider

Color quality list box

Screensavers

If you leave a static image displayed on an ordinary cathode-ray tube (CRT) monitor for too long, it's possible for that image to physically etch itself on the inside surface of your computer screen.

> **AS A MATTER OF FACT** *Liquid-crystal displays (LCDs) found on laptop computers and the latest LCD monitors never risk etching a static image on the screen. For LCD screens, screensavers serve as pure decoration.*

To prevent an image from physically etching itself on the inside of your monitor, Windows XP includes a special program called a screensaver. After a certain amount of inactivity, Windows XP runs the screensaver, which consists of an image that randomly appears in a different part of the screen.

To choose a screensaver and set the amount of time you want Windows XP to wait before it runs the screensaver, open the Display Properties dialog box and click the Screen Saver tab (see Figure 2-6).

Click in the Screen Saver list box and click the screensaver you want to use, such as Starfield or 3D Pipes.

> **AS A MATTER OF FACT** *If you choose the Marquee screensaver, you can type in text to appear on your screen instead of an image. If you choose the My Pictures Slideshow screensaver, Windows XP randomly displays a graphic image stored in your My Pictures folder.*

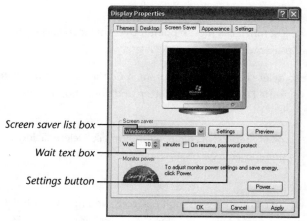

Figure 2-6
To create a screensaver, choose an image and the amount of time you want Windows XP to wait before it runs your screensaver.

Screen saver list box

Wait text box

Settings button

Click in the Wait text box and type the number of minutes you want Windows XP to wait before it runs your screensaver. If you choose too short a time, the screensaver may suddenly run in the middle of your work. Click OK when you're happy with your chosen screen saver.

AS A MATTER OF FACT *If you click the Preview button, you can see how your chosen screensaver works. Just tap a key or move the mouse to shut the screensaver off and return to the Display Properties dialog box again.*

Icons

Icons represent shortcuts to some, but not necessarily all, of the programs stored on your computer. So rather than click on the Start menu and then click the program you want to run, you can just click the icon that represents that program instead. Icons can represent either a program, a file created by a program such as a word processor, or a folder.

Delete

When you install a program for the first time, it may create its own icon on your desktop whether you want it there or not. Since your desktop may be cluttered with icons that you never use, the first way to customize your icons is to delete the icons you never use to avoid a cluttered desktop.

AS A MATTER OF FACT *When you delete an icon, you do not delete or modify the program that the icon represents.*

Delete One Icon

To delete a single icon, just move the mouse pointer over that icon and right-click the mouse. When a pop-up menu appears, click Delete.

If the icon you chose to delete represents a program, a Confirm Shortcut Delete dialog box appears. Click the Delete Shortcut button and your chosen icon disappears from view.

If the icon you chose to delete represents a file, a Confirm File Delete dialog box appears. Click Yes and your chosen icon disappears.

Delete Unused Icons

Since your desktop may get cluttered with multiple icons, you may want to let Windows XP automatically delete only those icons you rarely or never use. To delete these types of icons, right-click on any blank spot on the desktop (make sure you don't point the mouse pointer over an icon, the taskbar, or the Start button).

When a pop-up menu appears, move the mouse pointer over the **Arrange Icons By** command. Another pop-up menu appears. Click Run Desktop Cleanup Wizard.

The Desktop Cleanup Wizard dialog box appears. Click the Next button. The Desktop Cleanup Wizard dialog box lists all your icons and the dates you last used them. An X appears in the check box to the left of each icon that the Desktop Cleanup Wizard thinks you should delete. You can click in a check box to add an X or to remove an X from a check box next to an icon that you want to keep.

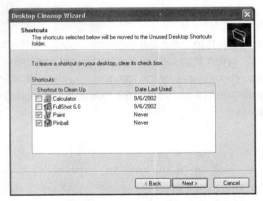

Figure 2-7

The Desktop Cleanup Wizard identifies seldom used and never used icons on your desktop.

Click the Next button. The Desktop Cleanup Wizard lists all the icons it plans to delete. (If you change your mind about deleting some of these icons, click the Back button). Otherwise, click the Finish button. Windows XP moves your chosen icons to a folder called Unused Desktop Shortcuts.

In case you want to retrieve an icon stored in the Unused Desktop Shortcuts folder, click the Start button, click **All Programs**, click **Accessories**, and click **Windows Explorer**.

Click the Unused Desktop Shortcuts folder to display all the icons stored in that folder. Right-click an icon so that a pop-up menu appears. Then move the mouse pointer over the **Send To** command so that another pop-up menu appears. Click **Desktop** (create shortcut). Windows XP puts your chosen icon back on the desktop. Click in the Close box of the Unused Desktop Shortcuts window to make it go away.

Add

If you find you use a particular program, file, or folder often, you may want to put a shortcut icon on your desktop. That way, the program or file will be just one click away, so you don't have to wade through the Start menu every time you want to load it.

To add a program or file, right-click on the desktop so that a pop-up menu appears. Move the mouse pointer over **New**, and when another pop-up menu appears, click **Shortcut**. A Create Shortcut dialog box appears. Click the Browse button. A Browse For Folder dialog box appears.

Figure 2-8
The Browse For Folder dialog box lets you choose a shortcut for a program, file, or folder.

If you want to browse through the different disks of your computer, click the plus sign that appears to the left of the My Computer icon. A list of drives appears underneath. Click the plus sign to the left of the drive you want to view to display all the folders stored on that drive.

Click a program name, file, or folder and then click OK. The Create Shortcut dialog box appears again with the name of your chosen folder. Click Next and type a descriptive name for your icon in the Type A Name For This Shortcut box. Then click Finish. Windows XP displays your chosen file or program as an icon on the desktop.

Rename

You can always change the names of your icons at any time. Just right-click the icon you want to rename and when a pop-up menu appears, click Rename. Windows XP highlights the current name of your icon. Just type a new name for your icon and when you're done, press **ENTER**.

Move

Windows XP organizes your icons according to the order you created them. If you'd rather rearrange your icons in a different order, move the mouse pointer over the icon you want to move, drag (hold down the left mouse button and move the mouse) until the icon is where you want it to be, and then let go of the mouse button.

To help you keep your icons arranged in neat rows and columns, Windows XP offers a special Align To Grid command. When you turn this command on, Windows XP always aligns your icons neatly. To turn on (or to turn off) the Align To Grid command, right-click on the desktop. When a pop-up menu appears, move the mouse pointer over **Arrange Icons By**, and when another pop-up menu appears, click **Align To Grid**. (If a check mark appears next to the Align To Grid command, that means you have already turned on this command.)

Rearrange

Sometimes you may want to rearrange all your icons at once, such as after you delete a bunch of unused icons using the Desktop Cleanup Wizard. Windows XP lets you rearrange your icons by Name, Size, Type, or Modified.

The Name option rearranges your icons alphabetically. Icons that start with the letter A appear closer to the upper left-hand corner of the screen. The Size option rearranges your icons by the size of the icon (not the size of the program, file, or folder the icon represents). Smaller icon sizes appear nearer the upper left-hand corner of the screen.

If you have several icons that represent files, you may want to group these icons together, such as all icons that represent word processor documents and all icons that represent web pages. To arrange your icons by type, choose the Type option.

The Modified option rearranges your icons according to the order you created or last changed them. (The oldest icon appears in the upper left-hand corner.)

To choose the Name, Size, Type, or Modified option, right-click on the desktop and when a pop-up menu appears, move the mouse pointer over **Arrange Icons By**. When another pop-up menu appears, click either **Name**, **Size**, **Type**, or **Modified**.

If you've deleted or moved so many icons that large gaps appear between several icons, you can tell Windows XP to rearrange all your icons automatically. This Auto-Arrange command simply closes the gaps between icons but doesn't change the order that the icons appear.

To use the Auto-Arrange command, right-click the desktop and when a pop-up menu appears, move the mouse pointer over **Arrange Icons By**. When another pop-up menu appears, click **Auto Arrange**.

AS A MATTER OF FACT *When you turn Auto-Arrange on, Windows XP won't let you leave any empty gaps between your icons if you move your icons around. If you want to leave gaps between your icons, choose the Auto-Arrange command again to turn it off.*

Hide

If you have too many icons that clutter up your desktop, you can choose to hide them temporarily from view rather than delete them. When you hide your icons, they disappear from view until you tell Windows XP to make them visible again.

To hide all your icons, right-click on the desktop and when a pop-up menu appears, move the mouse pointer over **Arrange Icons By**. When another pop-up menu appears, click **Show Desktop Icons**. Windows XP obediently hides all your icons from view.

When you want to display your hidden icons back on the desktop, just choose the **Show Desktop Icons** command again.

The Taskbar

The taskbar lets you start a new program and switch to a different program. Since you will use the taskbar every time you use your computer, Windows XP lets you modify its behavior and position on your screen to suit your preference.

Move

The taskbar normally appears at the bottom of the screen, but you can move it to the top, right, or left side of your screen at any time. To move the taskbar, move the mouse pointer over a blank part of the taskbar (make sure the mouse pointer doesn't point over an icon or button on the taskbar).

Drag the mouse (hold down the left mouse button and move the mouse) to the top, left, or right side of the screen. When the mouse pointer is close to one of the four edges of the screen, Windows XP displays your taskbar in its new location.

Hide

Normally the taskbar stays on the screen no matter how many programs you load, because Windows XP never knows if you might want to run or switch to another program. But sometimes you may want to hide the taskbar out of the way so that you can see more of your screen without the taskbar getting in the way. To hide the taskbar, Windows XP offers an Auto-Hide feature.

The Auto-Hide feature temporarily tucks the taskbar out of sight, but when you move the mouse near the taskbar, the taskbar slides back into place again. To turn on the Auto-Hide feature, right-click the taskbar and when a pop-up menu appears, click **Properties**. A Taskbar and Start Menu Properties dialog box appears. Click in the Auto-hide taskbar check box and click OK.

Figure 2-9

The Taskbar and Start Menu Properties dialog box lets you customize your taskbar.

Resize

As you load programs, the taskbar displays each program as a little button on the taskbar. Unfortunately, if you load too many programs, the taskbar squeezes each program button down in size so that all the buttons can appear on the taskbar, which can make each button hard to read.

To solve this problem, you can resize the taskbar so that more buttons can fit on it without getting squashed together. To resize your taskbar, move the mouse pointer over the top edge of the taskbar until the mouse pointer turns into a double-pointing arrow. (If you moved the taskbar to the top, left, or right side of the screen, move the mouse pointer over the inner edge of the taskbar, such as the right edge if the taskbar appears on the left side of your screen.)

When the mouse pointer turns into a double-pointing arrow, drag the mouse to resize the taskbar. When you're happy with the size of the taskbar, let go of the mouse button.

Group

Rather than resize your taskbar (and gobble up more of your screen in the process), you may want to group related buttons together. For example, if you have several different files open using Microsoft Word, the taskbar displays each Word document as a separate button on the taskbar. But if you choose the Group Similar Taskbar Buttons Together option, the taskbar lumps all related taskbar buttons as one as soon as the buttons on your taskbar start to get too crowded (see Figure 2-10).

So instead of showing several buttons representing multiple Word documents, the taskbar will now just show a single Microsoft Word button. When you click this single Microsoft Word button, a menu pops up that lists all the documents you currently have open.

Figure 2-10 *The taskbar can save space when it groups related programs together.*

To turn on the Group Similar Taskbar Buttons feature, right-click the taskbar and when a pop-up menu appears, click Properties. A Taskbar and Start Menu Properties dialog box appears. Click in the Group Similar Taskbar Buttons check box and click OK.

Lock

After you've customized all the changes to your taskbar, you may not want to mess it up accidentally. So to protect your taskbar, you can lock it. When you lock your taskbar, you simply prevent others (and yourself as well) from changing it.

To lock (or unlock) the taskbar, right-click the taskbar so that a menu pops up. Then click Lock The Taskbar.

AS A MATTER OF FACT   *After you have locked the taskbar, you won't be able to move, resize, or customize the taskbar again until you unlock it.*

Dates and Times

You should make sure you set your computer's clock so that Windows XP always knows the correct date and time. That way, if you create two copies of the same file and modify one of them, Windows XP will be able to tell you which file you modified last.

Date

To set your computer's date, double-click the clock that appears on the taskbar. A Date and Time Properties dialog box appears.

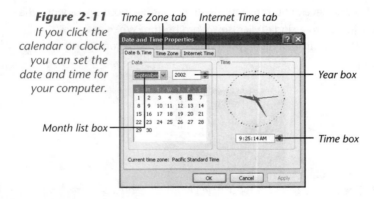

Figure 2-11
If you click the calendar or clock, you can set the date and time for your computer.

Time Zone tab   Internet Time tab

Year box

Month list box

Time box

To change the date, click in the Month list box and click the month. Click the up or down arrows of the Year box to display the correct year. Then click OK.

Time

To set your computer's clock, double-click the clock that appears on the taskbar. A Date And Time Properties dialog box appears.

To change the hour, double-click it in the Time box to highlight it. Then click the up or down arrow in the Time box to increase or decrease the number you highlighted. Repeat if necessary to modify the minutes or seconds. Then click OK.

Time Zone

Your computer has no idea what time zone you may be in, so you need to tell it. To set the time zone, double-click on the clock that appears on the taskbar. A Date And Time Properties dialog box appears.

Click the Time Zone tab and then click the time zone list box. Click the correct time zone that you are located in. If you want Windows XP to adjust automatically for daylight saving time, click in the Automatically Adjust Clock For Daylight Saving Changes check box and then click OK.

Format

If you don't like the way Windows XP displays the time or date, you can change it. For example, you may want to display the date the European way (day/month/year) or change the clock to military time (9:00 P.M. is 21:00).

To change the date and time format, click the Start button and click **Control Panel**. Click the Date, Time, Language, and Regional Options category. The Date, Time, Language, and Regional Options dialog box appears. Click Change the format of numbers, dates, and times. A Regional and Language Options dialog box appears.

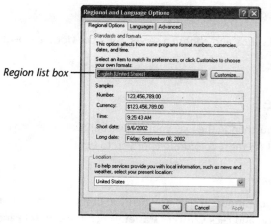

Region list box

Figure 2-12
You can define the format of your dates and time.

Click in the Region list box and click the region you want to use, such as English (United States) or French (France). When you choose a region, the dialog box displays the format of numbers so that you can see if this is what you really want. Click OK.

> **AS A MATTER OF FACT** *If you click the Customize button, you can set individual format preferences for how Windows XP displays dates, times, and numbers.*

Synchronize

Believe it or not, your computer clock loses track of time fairly easily, which means that after a while, the time could be off by as little as a minute or so or as much as an hour or more. To keep your computer's clock correct, you can tell Windows XP to synchronize your computer's clock with a time clock located on the Internet.

> **AS A MATTER OF FACT** *To synchronize the time on your computer, you must have an Internet connection. If you do not have an Internet connection, you won't be able to use this feature.*

To synchronize your computer's clock, double-click the clock that appears on the taskbar. A Date And Time Properties dialog box appears.

Click the Internet Time tab. Make sure a check mark appears in the Automatically Synchronize With An Internet Time Server check box. (If no check mark appears, click in that check box.)

Click in the Server list box and choose a server. Click the Update Now button and then click OK.

The Mouse

Windows XP lets you change the way your mouse behaves. That way, you can customize it so that it's most comfortable for you to work.

Clicking

To define the way your mouse responds when you press the mouse buttons down, click the Start button and click **Control Panel**. When the Control Panel window appears, click Printers and Other Hardware. Then click Mouse. A Mouse Properties dialog box appears (see Figure 2-13).

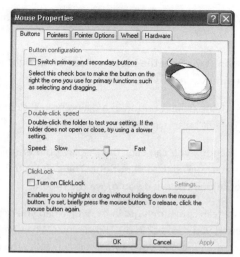

Figure 2-13
You can change the way your mouse responds.

Move the mouse pointer over the Speed slider and drag the mouse left or right to alter the double-click speed of your mouse. The closer you move the slider toward Fast, the faster you must double-click the left mouse button to give Windows XP a command. The closer you move the slider toward Slow, the slower you have to double-click to give Windows XP a command. After you move the Speed slider, you can double-click the folder icon to test your setting.

Normally when you drag the mouse, you have to hold down the left mouse button and move the mouse at the same time. If you find this too cumbersome, click in the Turn On ClickLock check box. When you turn on the ClickLock feature, you can click the left mouse button once, move the mouse, and click the left mouse button again as an alternative to the traditional method of dragging the mouse.

You can also switch the functions of the left and right mouse buttons if you click in the Switch Primary And Secondary Buttons check box. This can be particularly useful if you're left-handed.

When you're done changing your mouse properties, click OK. Then click the Close box of the Printers and Other Hardware window to make it go away.

Pointing

You can change the appearance of the mouse pointer if you click the Start button and then click **Control Panel**. When the Control Panel window appears, click Printers And Other Hardware. Then click Mouse. A Mouse Properties dialog box appears.

Click the Pointer tab. Then click the Scheme list box and choose a mouse scheme such as 3D-Bronze.

Click the Pointer Options tab. Drag the Motion slider left or right to modify how fast the mouse pointer moves across the screen.

To make it easier to click the default button in a dialog box, click in the Automatically move pointer to the default button in a dialog box check box.

Under the Visibility category, you can click the Display pointer trails check box and move the Display pointer trails slider left or right. The pointer trails feature makes it easier to find the mouse pointer when you move the mouse.

Since the mouse pointer can sometimes get in the way when you're using a program, such as a word processor, you can click in the Hide Pointer While Typing check box. That way, when you start typing, Windows XP temporarily hides the mouse pointer from view. When you move the mouse again, the mouse pointer will appear.

Finally, you may want to click in the Show Location Of Pointer When I Press The CTRL Key check box. That way, if you ever need to find the mouse pointer again, you can press the **CTRL** key and Windows XP will briefly display a circle around the mouse pointer to help you find it on your computer screen.

When you're done modifying your mouse properties, click OK and then click the Close box of the Printers And Other Hardware window to make it go away.

The Mouse Wheel

When you scroll the wheel button on your mouse, the wheel scrolls text up or down a fixed number of lines, such as three lines. To modify the number of lines that the wheel button scrolls text, click the Start button and then click **Control Panel**. When the Control Panel window appears, click Printers And Other Hardware. Then click Mouse. A Mouse Properties dialog box appears.

Click the Wheel tab. Click in the One Screen At A Time radio button. If you want to specify the number of lines you want the wheel button to scroll, click in the Following Lines At A Time text box and type a number.

When you're done, click OK and then click the Close box of the Printers And Other Hardware window to make it go away.

Conservation

If you have a laptop computer, you know that the batteries never seem to last long enough. So in an attempt to squeeze as much power out of a laptop computer's batteries as possible, Windows XP offers special power management features. (If you have a desktop computer, you can still take advantage of some of these power-saving features too. That way, your desktop computer consumes as little electricity as possible.)

Windows XP can save power by noticing when you've stopped using your computer for a specific period of time, such as ten minutes. After this time period passes, Windows XP assumes that you've stepped away from your computer and it can reduce or shut down power to your monitor and hard disk without turning off your computer completely. Then when you return, you can just tap a key or move the mouse and your computer springs back to life again.

To define how Windows XP conserves power, click the Start button and click **Control Panel**. In the Control Panel window, click Performance And Maintenance. Then click Power Options. A Power Options Properties dialog box appears.

Click in the Power Schemes list box and choose a power scheme, such as Portable/ Laptop. The dialog box displays your chosen options in the bottom half of the dialog box, showing how much time Windows XP waits before it shuts off the monitor, turns off your hard disk, puts your computer in standby mode, or puts your computer in hibernation mode.

Standby mode reduces power to your computer but allows you to restart it again quickly at the tap of a key or movement of the mouse. If you have any unsaved data, you may lose it if you don't save the data before you put the computer in standby mode.

Hibernation mode saves all your currently running programs and data to the hard disk temporarily and actually turns off your computer. When you activate a computer out of hibernation mode, it starts up again and displays all the programs and data that were in memory before you put it in hibernation mode. Restarting a computer out of hibernation mode is slower than standby mode, but without the risk of losing unsaved data as in standby mode.

Click in any of these list boxes to change the settings. Then click OK and click in the Close box of the Performance And Maintenance window to make it go away.

3

Organize Your Data

When you use Windows XP to run a program, you will eventually need to save some sort of data from that program, whether it's your high score in a video game, a letter from your word processor, your financial records from your money management program, or a digital photograph that you modified in your graphics program.

It's always easy to save data on your computer. It's just not always as easy to find that data again when you need it.

To help you find files that you may have stored somewhere on your computer last night, last week, or even last year, Windows XP provides a variety of ways to search for files by name, file type, or even by their contents. Now, you can store that important resume or incriminating letter on your computer and rest assured that you'll be able to find it again whenever you need it.

Besides helping you find files, Windows XP also gives you different ways to store, delete, rename, copy, and move your files. By learning how to organize your data easily and efficiently, you can get the most out of your computer and Windows XP without losing your mind in the process.

Save Files

Any time you choose the Save command from any program, that program stores your data inside your computer. Of course, your programs can't just save your data anywhere inside your computer. Specifically, programs must save your data on a drive, which is a generic term for any storage device attached to your computer such as a hard disk or a floppy disk.

A drive acts like a big closet for storing data from any program. While you could just toss data anywhere on a drive, you would likely have trouble finding that same data again. So to organize your data, you can divide a drive into little compartments called *folders*. A folder keeps data items separate from one another so that it's easier for you to find them again, much as dresser drawers keep your socks, shirts, and pants separate.

When you store data, your computer wraps your data in a neat little package called a *file*. A file can contain a single word, a drawing of your cat's face, a list of names and addresses, or an entire novel.

So every time you store data on your computer, your computer stores it as a file and tucks it inside a folder on a drive. To find data again, you need to remember which drive you saved it on, which folder you stored it in, and what name you gave your file when you saved it. (Don't worry. If you forget where you saved a file, Windows XP still has ways to help you find your files again.)

Files

Files represent chunks of information. To see how Windows XP can save a file, click the Start button and then click **All Programs**. When a menu pops up, click **Accessories** and then click **WordPad**. The WordPad program appears in a window on your screen.

Type **Big Brother is my friend.** Now click the **File** menu and click **Save**. A Save As dialog box appears (see Figure 3-1). (The Save As dialog box won't always look exactly the same in different programs.) Click in the File Name text box and type **Test File** for your filename.

> **AS A MATTER OF FACT** *Generally, you should give your files short, descriptive names such as "2003 finances" or "Ransom note." To avoid confusion, try not to use the same name for different files.*

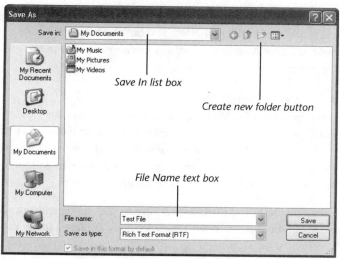

Figure 3-1 *When you save data for the first time, you must specify the drive, folder, and name for your file in the Save As dialog box.*

After you name your file, you still need to tell Windows XP where you want to store your file. To specify a drive, click in the Save In list box. A list appears, listing all the different drives available for your computer. Click the Local Disk (C:) drive. The Save As dialog box lists all the different folders on your chosen drive.

Click the folder where you want to store your file. Sometimes a folder may contain other folders, so you may need to click one or more additional folders until you find the one that you want. When you find the folder where you want to store your file, click the Save button. Then click the Close box in the WordPad window to make it go away.

> **AS A MATTER OF FACT** To help organize your files, Windows XP has created a My Documents folder on your computer so that you can store all your data there and find it easily by just looking in this one folder.

Folders

While you could store all your files on the same drive, you may want to group related files together. To group related files together, you can store them in a folder.

Folders can store files and even other folders. A folder usually has a descriptive name that gives you an idea of what type of files you've stored in that folder. For example, you might want to name a folder "Tax returns" or "Vacation pictures."

Although Windows XP has already created a folder called My Documents, you may want to create additional folders yourself. You can create folders in one of two ways: through the Save As dialog box of any program or through the Windows Explorer program.

Create a Folder Through Save As

When you want to save a file, you may not want to store it in any existing folders. Instead, you may want to create a new folder to store your data. To see how you can create a folder through the Save As dialog box, click the Start button and then click **All Programs**. When a menu pops up, click **Accessories** and then click **Paint**. The Paint program appears in a window on your screen.

Now click the **File** menu and click **Save**. A Save As dialog box appears. Click the Create New Folder button. Windows XP immediately displays a folder called New Folder with its name highlighted.

> **AS A MATTER OF FACT**   *If you want to create a folder in a different location, click the Look In list box and click the drive where you want to save your folder. Then click another folder if you want to save your folder inside another folder.*

Type a name for your folder and then press **ENTER** when you're done. Congratulations! You've just created a new folder. At this point, you could click your new folder, type a name for your file, and then click the Save button to save your file inside your new folder.

Click Cancel and then click the Close box of the Paint window to make the Paint window go away.

Create a Folder Through Windows Explorer

The Save As dialog box lets you create a new folder at the same time you're saving a new file. If you just want to create a new folder, you may find Windows Explorer easier to use instead.

To see how to create a folder with Windows Explorer, click the Start button and click My Computer (see Figure 3-2). The My Computer window appears. Double-click the drive where you want to create a new folder, such as on Local Disk (C:).

Click the **File** menu, click **New**, and then click **Folder**. Windows Explorer creates a new folder with the generic name New Folder.

Type **Junk Folder** and press **ENTER** to give your new folder a name. Now click the Close box of the Windows Explorer window to make it go away.

Back button   Forward button

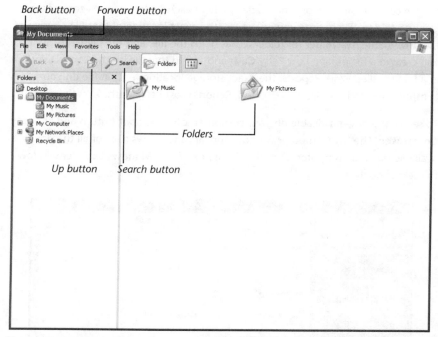

Figure 3-2 *Windows Explorer lets you see how you have organized your folders on your drives.*

AS A MATTER OF FACT *You can also create a new folder if you move the mouse pointer anywhere on the right panel (make sure it doesn't point over anything) and then right-click the mouse. When a pop-up menu appears, click* **New** *and then click* **Folder**.

Drives

Unlike when working with files and folders, you cannot create and save a drive. A drive represents a physical device that's attached to your computer. The most common drives in every computer are a floppy disk, a hard disk, and a CD drive.

To identify each drive, Windows XP gives each drive a unique name (such as 3½ Floppy) along with a letter designation (such as A:). (Just in case you're wondering, computers used to have two floppy drives, so the first one would be called A: and the second B:. Since most computers now only have one floppy drive, the first floppy drive is called A: and there is usually no B: drive.)

A drive can contain zero or more folders, where each folder contains zero or more files and folders. Every time you save a file, the exact location of that file consists of the drive name, the folder (or folders) that holds the file, and the filename. So if you created a file named Lost Petty Cash and stored that file on the Local Disk (C:) in a folder called Work Reports, the exact storage location for that file on your computer would look like this: C:\Work Reports\Lost Petty Cash.

To see all the drives available on your computer, click the Start button and click **My Computer**. The My Computer window appears and shows a list of all the drives available on your computer. Click the Close box of the Windows Explorer window to make it go away.

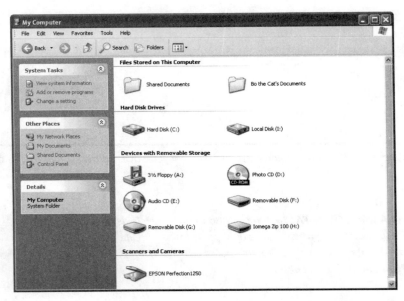

Figure 3-3 *The My Computer window lets you see all the drives on your computer.*

Find Files

After you've stored a file somewhere inside your computer, you can use Windows Explorer to help you find it again. To find a file, you just need to know part or all of the name you gave your file.

The two most common files you may need to find are documents and multimedia files. A *document* is a generic term for any data that consists of text, such as any file created by a word processor, a spreadsheet, or a database. A multimedia file is any file that contains graphics, sound, or video.

Search by Name

To see how to find a file with Windows Explorer, click the Start button and click **All Programs**. Click **Accessories** and when a pop-up menu appears, click **WordPad**. The WordPad window appears.

Type **You found me!** Click the **File** menu and then click **Save**. A Save As dialog box appears. Type **Garbage** in the File Name box and click Save. Now click the Close box of the WordPad window to make it go away.

Click the Start button and click **All Programs**. Click **Accessories** and then click **Windows Explorer**. The Windows Explorer window appears.

Click the Search button. The Search Companion appears in the left pane of Windows Explorer and asks you what type of file you want to find (see Figure 3-4). Click Documents (word processing, spreadsheets, etc.).

Windows Explorer asks you when you last modified the file you want to find. Click the Within The Last Week radio button. Now click in the Document Name box and type **GAR**. Click the Search button.

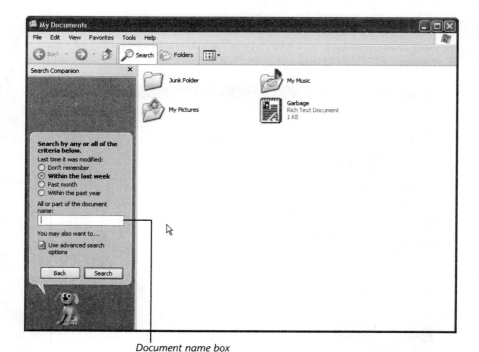

Document name box

Figure 3-4 *Windows Explorer can help you find a document you've lost on your computer.*

Within a minute or two, Windows Explorer displays all the files that contain the letters GAR in their names. Click Yes, Finished Searching. Now double-click the Garbage file and WordPad obediently loads and displays the file contents for you.

Click the Close box of the WordPad window and the Close box of Windows Explorer to make them go away.

Search by File Contents

Sometimes you may not remember the name of the file you want to find, but you do remember some of the words stored in the file you want to find. To find a file based on its contents, click the Start button and click **All Programs**. When a pop-up menu appears, click **Accessories** and then click **Windows Explorer**. The Windows Explorer window appears.

Click the Search button. The Search Companion appears in the left pane of Windows Explorer and asks you what type of file you want to find. Click All Files And Folders.

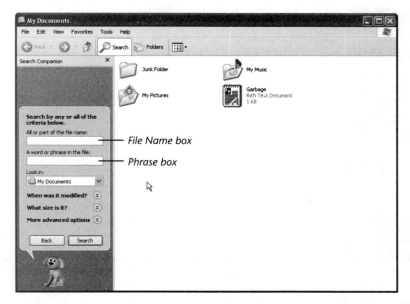

Figure 3-5 *Windows Explorer can search for a file according to its contents.*

Click in the Phrase box and type **You found me!** Then click the Search button. Windows Explorer displays the Garbage file you created in the preceding section. Click the Garbage file and WordPad obediently loads and displays the file contents for you. Click the Close box of the WordPad window and the Close box of Windows Explorer to make them go away.

Find a Multimedia File

To see how to find a multimedia (picture, sound, video) file with Windows Explorer, click the Start button and click **All Programs**. Click **Accessories**, and when a pop-up menu appears, click **Paint**. The Paint window appears.

Drag the mouse (hold down the left mouse button and move the mouse) around the screen to draw a picture. (If nothing appears when you drag the mouse, click the Pencil icon on the left-hand side of the Paint window and then drag the mouse around the screen.)

Click the **File** menu and then click **Save**. A Save As dialog box appears. Type **Graffiti** in the File Name box and then click Save. Click the Close box of the Paint window to make it go away.

Now click the Start button and click **All Programs**. When a pop-up menu appears, click **Accessories** and then click **Windows Explorer**. The Windows Explorer window appears.

Click the Search button. The Search Companion appears in the left pane of Windows Explorer and asks you what type of file you want to find. Click Pictures, Music, or Video. Click the Pictures And Photos check box and then click in the File Name box. Type **Graffiti** and then click the Search button. Windows Explorer displays your Graffiti file.

Double-click the Graffiti file. The Windows Picture And Fax Viewer window appears. Click the Close box of this window to make it go away. Click Yes, Finished Searching in the Windows Explorer window and then click in the Close box of the Windows Explorer window to make it go away.

Browse Files

You can use Windows Explorer every time you want to see how you have organized data on your computer. Windows Explorer can show you how many drives your computer has, the names of all the folders stored on each drive (and inside each folder too if you have stored a folder inside another folder), and the names of all the files stored on all your drives and inside each folder.

Windows Explorer gives you two different ways to display the drives, folders, and files stored on your computer. The first method lists a menu of tasks on the left side of the Windows Explorer window and displays your drives, folders, and files in the right side of the window.

The second method lists all the drives and folders on your computer in a hierarchical outline on the left side of the Windows Explorer window. When you click a drive or folder on the left side of this window, the right side of the window displays the contents of that drive or folder.

Display Tasks

With the tasks displayed on the left side of Windows Explorer, you can always see a list of commands you can choose at any time. The drawback comes when you want to see the contents of a different drive. To view another drive, you have to click the Up button one or more times until you see a list of all the drives available on your computer.

To see how cumbersome this method can be, right-click the Start button. When a pop-up menu appears, click **Explore**. Windows Explorer appears and displays the contents of a folder called Start Menu.

If you don't see a list of tasks in the left side of the Windows Explorer window, click the Folders button.

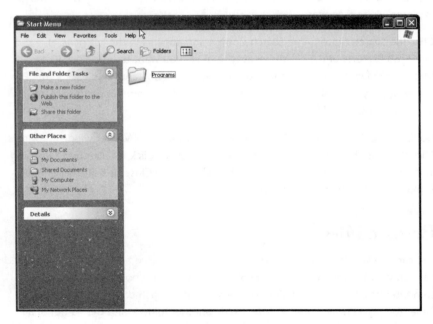

Figure 3-6 *Windows Explorer can display a list of tasks in the left side of the window.*

Click the Up button. Windows Explorer displays the contents of a new folder. The specific folder name appears in the title bar of the Windows Explorer window. Click the Up button again and notice that the title bar displays the name of another folder while the Windows Explorer window displays the contents of that particular folder.

Click the Up button again. The title bar displays the name of the drive you're viewing, which is Local Disk (C:). Click the Up button one more time. Windows Explorer finally shows you a list of all the drives available on your computer.

Click the Close box of the Windows Explorer window to make it go away.

Display Folders

Rather than fill the left side of the window with a list of commands, Windows Explorer can display a hierarchical list of all the drives and folders on your computer. When you click a drive or folder on the left side of the Windows Explorer window, you can see the contents of that drive or folder on the right side of the window.

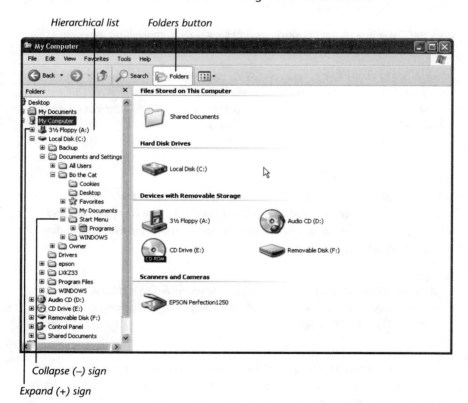

Hierarchical list   *Folders button*

Collapse (–) sign

Expand (+) sign

Figure 3-7   *Windows Explorer can display a hierarchical list of your drives and folders.*

At first, deciphering the cryptic appearance of this hierarchic list may be intimidating, but once you understand how it works, it can be a much faster way to switch drives and folders to view. Whenever an Expand (+) sign appears to the left of a drive or folder, that means there are more folders temporarily hidden from view. If you click the Expand (+) sign, Windows Explorer shows you those hidden folders.

In case the hierarchical list gets too cluttered, click the Collapse (–) sign that appears to the left of each drive or folder. If there is no Expand (+) or Collapse (–) sign next to a drive or folder, that means there are no folders hidden from view.

To see how this hierarchical list works, right-click the Start button. When a pop-up menu appears, click **Explore**. Windows Explorer appears and displays the contents of a folder called Start Menu. (If you cannot see this hierarchical list, click the Folders button.) The hierarchical list lets you see all the drives and folders available on your computer. Click the Collapse (–) sign to the left of the Local Disk (C:). Windows Explorer collapses the list of folders stored on the Local Disk (C:) and displays the Expand (+) sign to the left.

Click the Close box of the Windows Explorer window to make it go away.

AS A MATTER OF FACT *You can always combine the two methods to get the best of both worlds. For example, view the hierarchical list to switch to a drive or folder quickly, and then click the Folders button to make the hierarchical list go away and display a list of tasks you can choose.*

Customize Views

Windows Explorer can display your files and folders in five different ways: thumbnails, tiles, icons, list, and details (see Figure 3-8). The way your files and folders appear in Windows Explorer is just for your personal preference and does not physically alter your files in any way.

AS A MATTER OF FACT *You can define different folders to display icons in different ways. For example, one folder can display icons as thumbnails and a second folder can display icons as tiles.*

Thumbnails displays your files and folders in large icons, which make them easier to read and find, but if you have many files or folders, the large size of thumbnails means that some files or folders may be hidden from view.

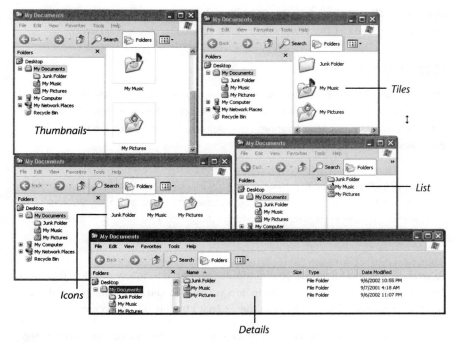

Figure 3-8 *Windows Explorer can display your files and folders in several different ways.*

Tiles display icons in neatly aligned rows and columns. Tiles display icons in a much smaller size than thumbnails, which makes tiles a good choice for displaying multiple items in Windows Explorer.

Icons display files and folders as smaller icons in rows and columns. This choice is also good for displaying multiple items in Windows Explorer.

Lists display files and folders as tiny icons in rows and columns. This choice can be best for displaying a large number of items in Windows Explorer.

Details display files and folders in a single column as small icons, much like the Lists option. The difference is that the Details option displays the size, type, and last date modified of each file and folder.

To see these different views, click the Start button and click **All Programs**. When a menu pops up, click **Accessories** and then click **Windows Explorer**. The Windows Explorer window appears.

Click the **View** menu. A pull-down menu appears, listing the **Thumbnails**, **Tiles**, **Icons**, **List**, and **Details** options. Click **Thumbnails**. Then click the **View** menu and choose **Tiles**. Repeat this process until you've chosen **Icons**, **List**, and **Details**. Click the Close box of the Windows Explorer window to make it go away.

Arrange Files

After you store enough files on your computer, you may later decide that you need to copy, move, rename, or delete some of the files or folders you created. Whenever you want to arrange (and rearrange) your files and folders, you have to use Windows Explorer.

> **AS A MATTER OF FACT**   *Unlike most programs such as a word processor or a database, Windows Explorer doesn't create any data to store in a file. Instead, Windows Explorer simply lets you rearrange data that other programs have stored in a file.*

To arrange files and folders on your computer, you have to follow a two-step process. First, you have to select the files and folders you want to arrange. This essentially tells Windows Explorer, "See this file right there? That's the one I want to move."

Once you have told Windows Explorer what you want to arrange, the second step involves giving Windows Explorer an actual command to tell it what to do, such as copy, move, delete, or rename the file or folder.

Select Files

You can select one or more files or folders at once. That way, you can copy, move, or delete a group of files or folders all at the same time.

Customize

Windows XP gives you two ways to select a file or folder: point to select or click to select. The point to select option means you can move the mouse pointer over the file or folder you want to select, wait a second or two, and Windows Explorer automatically selects whatever the mouse points at. This method can be fast, but it may accidentally select files or folders that you didn't want to select, simply because you left the mouse pointer over a file or folder for too long.

The click to select option won't select anything until you specifically click that item. This can prevent accidentally selecting a file or folder, but it isn't as fast or convenient as simply pointing at a file or folder to select it.

To choose either the point to select or click to select option, click the Start button and click **All Programs**. When a menu pops up, click **Accessories** and then click **Windows Explorer**. The Windows Explorer window appears.

Click the **Tools** menu and click **Folder Options**. A Folder Options dialog box appears.

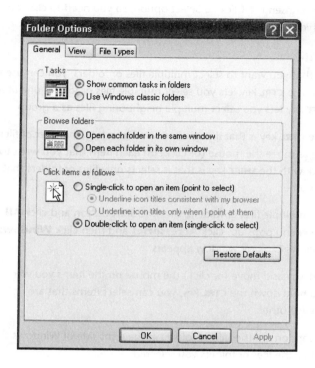

Figure 3-9
The Folder Options dialog box lets you choose between the point to select and the click to select commands.

Click either the Single-Click To Open An Item radio button or the Double-Click To Open An Item radio button. (If you chose the Single-Click To Open An Item radio button, you can also choose two additional radio buttons: Underline Icon Titles Consistent With My Browser or Underline Icon Titles Only When I Point At Them.) Click OK. Click the Close box of the Windows Explorer window to make it go away.

AS A MATTER OF FACT *The options you choose in the Folder Options dialog box also changes the way the Open dialog box works in every program on your computer. Thus, if you choose the Single-Click To Open An Item radio button, every time you choose the Open command in a program, that program lets you select a file to open with just a single click.*

Select One Item

To see how to select a single file or folder, click the Start button and click **All Programs**. When a list pops up, click **Accessories** and then click **Windows Explorer**. The Windows Explorer window appears.

To select a file or folder, move the mouse pointer over that file or folder until Windows Explorer highlights it. (If Windows Explorer doesn't highlight the item, that means you have chosen the Click To Select option, so you need to click on the file or folder to highlight it.)

Select Two or More

To tell Windows XP that you want to select multiple files or folders, you can use the **CTRL** and **SHIFT** keys. The **CTRL** key lets you select multiple files or folders one at a time, while the **SHIFT** key lets you select multiple neighboring files as a group.

The drawback of the **CTRL** key is that if you want to select a large number of files or folders, you have to move the mouse (or click) on each item that you want to select. The drawback with the **SHIFT** key is that it selects only files or folders that appear next to each other.

To see how to select multiple files or folders, click the Start button and click **All Programs**. When a menu pops up, click **Accessories** and then click **Windows Explorer**. The Windows Explorer window appears.

Hold down the **CTRL** key and move (or click) the mouse on the items you want to select. When you hold down the **CTRL** key, you can select items that are not necessarily next to each other.

Click anywhere (except on another file or folder) in the right side of Windows Explorer to deselect all the files or folders you selected.

To see how the **SHIFT** key lets you select multiple files or folders that are next to each other, move (or click) the mouse pointer over a file or folder. Windows Explorer highlights that file or folder.

Now hold the **SHIFT** key down and move (or click) the mouse pointer over another file or folder far away from the first file or folder you selected. Windows Explorer highlights this file or folder along with any files or folders in between.

Click anywhere (except on another file or folder) in the right side of Windows Explorer to deselect all the files or folders you selected.

For another way to select a group of neighboring files or folders, you can just use the mouse by itself without the keyboard. Move the mouse to the side of the first file or folder you want to select (do not move the mouse pointer directly over this item). Now drag the mouse (hold down the left mouse button and move the mouse) over the other items you want to select. As you drag the mouse, Windows Explorer draws a box. Anything that this box covers gets selected (see Figure 3-10).

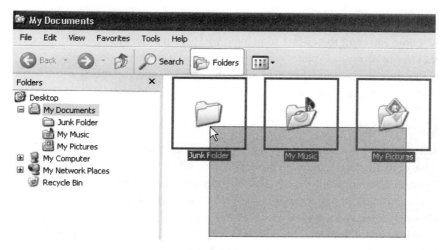

Figure 3-10 *When you drag the mouse over items you want to select, Windows XP displays a rectangle on the screen.*

Click anywhere (except on another file or folder) in the right side of Windows Explorer to deselect all the files or folders you selected.

AS A MATTER OF FACT *You can always use both methods to select multiple items. For example, you might want to drag the mouse over multiple items and then hold* **CTRL** *as you click additional files or folders to select.*

Select Everything

If you want to select everything, Windows Explorer offers a special Select All command. To see how to select everything stored in a folder, click the Start button and click **All Programs**. When a list pops up, click **Accessories** and then click **Windows Explorer**. The Windows Explorer window appears.

Press **CTRL-A**. Windows Explorer highlights everything in the right side of the Windows Explorer window.

AS A MATTER OF FACT *If you want to select a large number of items, you can use two shortcuts. First, you can press* **CTRL-A** *to select everything and then hold the* **CTRL** *key while you click the items you don't want to select. As an alternative, hold down the* **CTRL** *key and select all the items you don't want to select. Then click* **Edit** *and then click* **Inverse Selection***. Now Windows Explorer only highlights everything you did not select initially.*

Deselect

Any time you want to deselect something you have selected, just click on any blank spot in the Windows Explorer window. In case you want to deselect certain items but keep others selected, just hold down the **CTRL** key and click the selected items that you now want to deselect.

Copy Files

After you have selected a file or folder, you can copy that file or folder to another drive or in a different folder on the same drive. When you copy a file and store it in a new location, Windows XP saves the duplicate copy with the same name as the original file. So if you copy a file named "Cat Food Recipes" and store it in a different folder, you will now have two files named "Cat Food Recipes." If you modify either or both files, it's possible that both files can contain completely different data yet still have the identical filename.

> **AS A MATTER OF FACT** *Be careful about making too many copies of files or folders. If you modify two different copies of the same file, you will have duplicate, but slightly different versions of each file and you may not remember which file contains the most accurate data.*

If you copy a file and store it in the same location as the original file, Windows XP gives the copy a new name. So if you copy a file named "Radiation Tests" and store that copy in the same folder as the original file, Windows XP would name the duplicate file "Copy of Radiation Tests." (If you create yet another copy of that file and store it in the same folder as the original file, Windows XP gives each additional copy a number as part of its name such as "Copy (2) of Radiation Tests" or "Copy (3) of Radiation Tests.")

Copy Files

To see how to copy a single file, click the Start button and click **All Programs**. When a list pops up, click **Accessories** and then click **Windows Explorer**. The Windows Explorer window appears.

Double-click the My Pictures folder. Windows Explorer displays the contents of the My Pictures folder. Double-click the Sample Pictures folder. Right-click over the Sunset file. When a pop-up menu appears, click **Copy**.

Right-click anywhere on the right side of the Windows Explorer window. (Make sure the mouse pointer isn't pointing over anything.) When a pop-up menu appears, click **Paste**. Windows Explorer creates a copy of your chosen file and names it Copy of Sunset. (If you had copied the file to a different folder or drive, Windows XP would have named it Sunset, without the words "Copy of" in the first part of the name.)

Click the Close box of the Windows Explorer window to make it go away.

Copy Folders

When you copy a folder, Windows XP also copies any files currently stored inside that folder. To copy a folder, click the Start button and click **All Programs**. When a list pops up, click **Accessories** and then click **Windows Explorer**. The Windows Explorer window appears.

Right-click the My Pictures folder. When a pop-up menu appears, click **Copy**. Right-click anywhere (but over another file or folder) in the right side of the Windows Explorer window and when a pop-up menu appears, click **Paste**.

Windows Explorer creates a copy of the My Pictures folder and names it Copy of My Pictures. (If you had copied the folder to a different folder or drive, Windows XP would have named it My Pictures, without the words "Copy of" in the first part of the name.) If you open the Copy of My Pictures and the original My Pictures folder, you'll see that they contain identical files.

Click the Close box of the Windows Explorer window to make it go away.

Copy to a Removable Drive

Since many people copy files onto a removable disk (such as a floppy disk) so that they can transfer the files to another computer, Windows XP offers a special copy command called the Send To command.

When you use the Send To command, Windows XP displays a list of all the removable drives where you can copy a file or folder. To see how the Send To command works, click the Start button and click **All Programs**. When a list pops up, click **Accessories** and then click **Windows Explorer**. The Windows Explorer window appears.

Right-click a file or folder. When a pop-up menu appears, click **Send To**. Another menu pops up, showing you all the removable drives where you can copy your file or folder (see Figure 3-11). Click the Close box of the Windows Explorer window to make it go away.

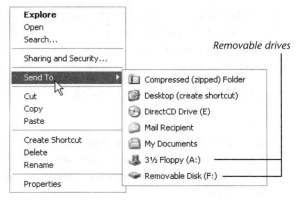

Figure 3-11
The Send To command can copy a file or folder to a removable drive.

Explore
Open
Search...

Sharing and Security...

Send To

Cut
Copy
Paste

Create Shortcut
Delete
Rename

Properties

Removable drives

Compressed (zipped) Folder
Desktop (create shortcut)
DirectCD Drive (E)
Mail Recipient
My Documents
3½ Floppy (A:)
Removable Disk (F:)

AS A MATTER OF FACT *When you choose the Send To command, a menu pops up that lists removable drives along with other places where you can copy your chosen file or folder. Windows XP identifies removable drives by displaying a letter enclosed in parentheses such as (C:) or (E:).*

Move Files

When you copy a file or folder, you have to worry about multiple copies of the same files becoming scattered across your hard disk. Rather than copy a file or folder, just move it instead. Windows XP gives you two ways to move a file or folder: cut an item and paste it in a new location or drag the item to a new location.

AS A MATTER OF FACT *Be careful about moving files or folders to a removable drive such as a floppy disk because if you misplace that disk, you won't have a backup copy of your files or folders stored on your hard disk.*

Cut and Paste

The cut and paste method to move a file involves multiple steps, so it's not very fast, but it is easy to learn. To see how to cut and paste a file to move it, click the Start button and click **All Programs**. When a list pops up, click **Accessories** and then click **Windows Explorer**. The Windows Explorer window appears.

Double-click the My Pictures folder to display the folder contents and then double-click the Sample Pictures folder. Right-click the Sunset file and when a pop-up menu appears, click **Cut**. Windows dims the Sunset file.

Click the Up button. Now move the mouse pointer anywhere to the right of the Windows Explorer window (make sure the mouse pointer doesn't point over a file

or folder) and right-click. When a pop-up menu appears, click **Paste**. Windows
Explorer displays the Sunset file in its new location.

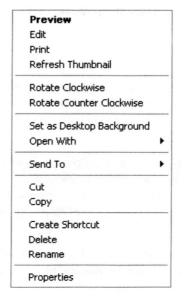

Preview
Edit
Print
Refresh Thumbnail
Rotate Clockwise
Rotate Counter Clockwise
Set as Desktop Background
Open With ▶
Send To ▶
Cut
Copy
Create Shortcut
Delete
Rename
Properties

Figure 3-12
*When you
right-click an
item, a pop-up
menu displays
commands to cut,
copy, rename, or
delete a file or
folder.*

Click the **Edit** menu and click **Undo Move**. Click the Close box of the Windows
Explorer window to make it go away.

Drag

A faster way to move a file or folder involves dragging the mouse. The drawback of
this method is that it's easy to move a file or folder to the wrong location by mistake,
especially if you're not that comfortable using the mouse.

To see how to move a file by dragging the mouse, click the Start button and click
All Programs. When a list pops up, click **Accessories** and then click **Windows
Explorer**. The Windows Explorer window appears.

Double-click the My Pictures folder to display the folder contents and double-click
the Sample Pictures folder. If you can't see the hierarchical list in the left side of the
window, click the Folders button.

Move the mouse pointer over the Sunset file in the right side of the window and
drag the mouse (hold down the left mouse button and move the mouse) over to
the My Music folder displayed in the hierarchical list on the left side of the window.
When the My Music folder appears highlighted, release the left mouse button. The
Sunset file disappears from view.

Double-click the My Music folder in the hierarchical list. Windows Explorer displays the contents of the My Music folder, which includes the Sunset file that you just moved.

Click the **Edit** menu and click **Undo Move**. Click the Close box of the Windows Explorer window to make it go away.

Rename Files

In case you don't like the original name you (or someone else) gave to a file, you can always change a file's name at any time. You can rename a file whenever you see that file displayed in either Windows Explorer or an Open dialog box within any program.

> **AS A MATTER OF FACT** *Many programs keep track of the last files you opened, so if you want to open a recently modified file, you can choose from the list of recently opened files. But be careful, because if you rename a file, this list of recently opened files will no longer work for your renamed file.*

To see how to rename a file or folder, click the Start button and click **All Programs**. When a list pops up, click **Accessories** and then click **Windows Explorer**. The Windows Explorer window appears.

Double-click the My Pictures folder to view the contents of that folder and double-click the Sample Pictures folder. Right-click the Sunset file and when a pop-up menu appears, click **Rename**. Windows XP highlights the filename. Type **Just a Test**, and then press **ENTER**. Windows XP displays your new name for your chosen file.

> **AS A MATTER OF FACT** *Rather than type an entirely new name, you can edit the existing name of a file. Just use the LEFT ARROW and RIGHT ARROW keys and press the BACKSPACE key to delete any character to the left of the cursor.*

Click the **Edit** menu and click **Undo Rename**. Click the Close box of the Windows Explorer window to make it go away.

Examine Files

When you look at a file or folder in the Windows Explorer window, you may have no idea how large that file or folder may be, the date you created that file, or the date you last modified that file.

To view this information, you can view the properties of any file or folder. To view the properties of a folder, click the Start button and click **All Programs**. When a list pops up, click **Accessories** and then click **Windows Explorer**. The Windows Explorer window appears.

Right-click the My Pictures folder. When a pop-up menu appears, click **Properties**. Windows XP displays a properties dialog box that lists the size of the file or folder and the date you created it (see Figure 3-13). (If you view the properties of a file, the Properties dialog box will also tell you the date you last modified that file.)

Click OK. Then click the Close box of the Windows Explorer window to make it go away.

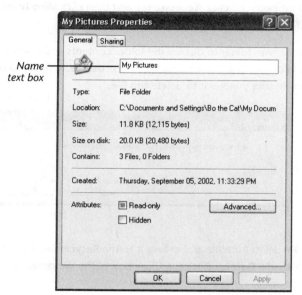

Name text box

Figure 3-13
The Properties dialog box shows you the details about a file or folder.

> **AS A MATTER OF FACT** *If you click in the Name text box, you can rename (edit the name of) your file or folder.*

Delete Files

After you use your computer for a while, you may find that you no longer need files that you created long ago, such as a love letter you once wrote to someone who is now an ex-spouse. Rather than clutter up your hard disk with useless files, get rid of them.

> **AS A MATTER OF FACT** *When you delete a file, Windows XP really just moves it into a special folder called the Recycle Bin. That way, if you suddenly decide you need a deleted file after all, you can retrieve it from the Recycle Bin.*

Windows XP gives you two ways to delete a file: through the **DELETE** key on your keyboard or through your mouse.

The Delete Key

To delete a file or folder, you need to run the Windows Explorer program and then select the file or folder that you want to delete. Then press **DELETE** (abbreviated on some keyboards as **del**).

To see how to delete a file with the **DELETE** key, click the Start button and click **All Programs**. When a list pops up, click **Accessories** and then click **Windows Explorer**. The Windows Explorer window appears.

Double-click the My Pictures folder to display the folder contents and double-click the Sample Pictures folder. Click the Sunset file and press **DELETE**. A dialog box appears, asking if you're sure you want to delete this file.

Figure 3-14
Windows XP asks
for confirmation
before you
delete a file.

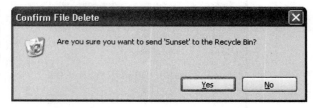

Click Yes. Windows XP deletes the file and moves it to the Recycle Bin. Click the **Edit** menu and click **Undo Delete**. Click the Close box of the Windows Explorer window to make it go away.

Right-Click Delete

A more versatile method to delete a file uses the mouse. Any time you see a file displayed either in Windows Explorer or in the Open dialog box of any program, right-click the file that you want to delete. When a pop-up menu appears, click **Delete**. A dialog box appears, asking if you're sure you want to delete this file. Click Yes.

To see how you can use the right-click method in an Open dialog box, click the Start button and click **All Programs**. When a list pops up, click **Accessories** and then click **Notepad**. The Notepad window appears.

Click File and then click Open. When the Open dialog box appears, right-click a file or folder. A pop-up menu appears. If you want to delete this file, click Delete. Otherwise, press **ESC** to make the pop-up menu go away. Then click Cancel to make the Open dialog box go away. Finally, click in the Close box of the Notepad window to make the Notepad window go away.

Undo Delete

Nothing is worse than to delete a file and suddenly realize that you need that file after all. So if you delete a file and suddenly change your mind, you can recover your file if you immediately choose the Undo command.

> **AS A MATTER OF FACT**   *The Undo Delete command works only if you immediately choose this command after you delete a file or folder. If you delete a file or folder, do something else, and then suddenly decide you want to retrieve a deleted file or folder, you won't be able to use the Undo Delete command. In this case, you will have to retrieve the deleted file or folder from the Recycle Bin.*

To see how the Undo command can retrieve a file you just deleted, click the Start button and click **All Programs**. When a menu pops up, click **Accessories** and then click **Notepad**. The Notepad window appears.

Click **File** and then click **Open**. When the Open dialog box appears, right-click any file or folder. When a pop-up menu appears, click **Delete**. When a dialog box appears to ask if you really want to delete this file or folder, click Yes.

Now to retrieve this file, press **CTRL-Z**, or right-click anywhere in the Open dialog box (except over another file or folder) and when a pop-up menu appears, click **Undo Delete**.

Windows XP immediately returns the file or folder you deleted. Click Cancel to make the Open dialog box go away. Then click the Close box of the Notepad window to make the Notepad window go away.

Retrieve from Recycle Bin

If you have deleted a file or folder, you can always retrieve it again from the Recycle Bin. To see how you can retrieve a file, click the Start button and click **All Programs**. When a menu pops up, click **Accessories** and then click **Windows Explorer**. The Windows Explorer window appears.

> **AS A MATTER OF FACT**   *When you retrieve an item from the Recycle Bin, Windows XP simply moves the file or folder out from the Recycle Bin to the preceding location of the file or folder.*

Double-click the My Pictures folder and then double-click the Sample Pictures folder. Click the Sunset file and press **DELETE**. When a dialog box appears to ask if you really want to delete this file, click Yes.

If you cannot see the hierarchical list, click the Folders button. Click the Recycle Bin icon. The right side of the Windows Explorer window displays all the files currently stored in the Recycle Bin. Right-click the file you want to retrieve, such as the Sunset file.

When a pop-up menu appears, click **Restore**. Windows XP moves the file to its preceding location.

Empty the Recycle Bin

You could leave all your deleted files in the Recycle Bin to retrieve again in an emergency. Unfortunately, any files stored in the Recycle Bin take up room, and eventually your deleted files can gobble up precious hard disk space. So when you're absolutely sure you won't need a particular file, it's better to delete that file or folder for good, which is called emptying the Recycle Bin.

To empty the Recycle Bin, right-click the Recycle Bin icon on your desktop. (You may need to click the Close box of any window that appears on your screen.) When a menu pops up, click **Empty Recycle Bin**.

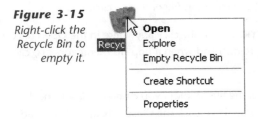

Figure 3-15
Right-click the Recycle Bin to empty it.

| Open |
| Explore |
| Empty Recycle Bin |
| Create Shortcut |
| Properties |

A dialog box appears, asking if you really want to delete all the files and folders stored in the Recycle Bin. Click Yes.

4

Connect

Although you can use Windows XP to run games, type letters, or play music, chances are good that one day you'll want to connect your computer to the Internet. Connecting your computer to the Internet isn't difficult, and once you're connected, you can shop online, read the latest news, and exchange e-mail with people all over the world. Think of the Internet as a massive collection of information that you can peek at using your computer at any time.

Some people use the Internet to research and shop through different Web sites. Other people use the Internet to send and receive e-mail from friends, relatives, and co-workers all over the world. Still others enjoy exchanging messages through newsgroups where people can discuss specific hobbies or activities like skiing, gardening, computer programming, or football.

The Internet can open up a whole new world for you to explore, meet new people, and keep in touch with anyone no matter where they might live or work. But first you have to learn how to connect to the Internet through Windows XP, and this chapter shows you how.

Preparing to Connect

To connect to the Internet, you need a physical connection to the Internet (such as a telephone line) and an account with a company known as an Internet service provider (ISP), which acts as a tollbooth that grants you access to the Internet in exchange for a fee. Some popular ISPs include America Online (AOL), the Microsoft Network (MSN), and EarthLink, although there are literally thousands of ISPs you can choose from with varying price ranges, reliability, and support.

The two most common ways to connect to the Internet are dial-up and broadband access. Dial-up access means you connect to the Internet through an ordinary telephone line and a phone modem, while broadband access means you connect through a DSL (digital subscriber line) or cable modem.

If you use dial-up access, you must dial a local telephone number every time you want to access the Internet. If you use broadcast access, your computer remains connected to the Internet at all times. To connect your computer to the Internet, you need specific information from your particular ISP, which varies from one ISP to another.

To configure your computer for dial-up Internet access, you must know your account name or ID, your password, and an access number you need to call to connect to the Internet. When you configure your computer for broadband access, you may need to type in specific network settings.

To see what steps you may need to set up a dial-up access Internet connection, click the Start button and then click **Control Panel**. When the Control Panel window appears, click Network And Internet Connections. When the Network And Internet Connections window appears, click Set Up Or Change Your Internet Connection. The Internet Properties dialog box appears.

Figure 4-1
The Internet Properties dialog box lets you set up your computer to connect to the Internet through dial-up or broadband access.

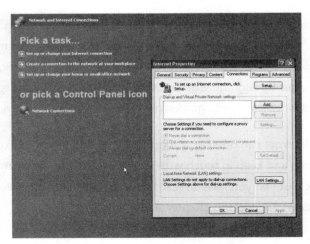

Click Add. A New Connection Wizard dialog box appears that asks how you want to connect to the Internet.

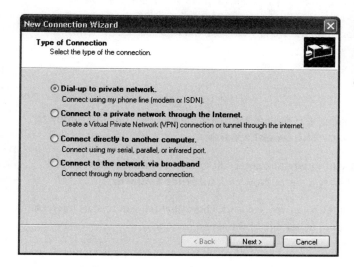

Figure 4-2
You can connect to the Internet through a variety of methods.

AS A MATTER OF FACT *If you sign up with America Online, the figures and instructions in this chapter won't work exactly the same on your computer.*

Click a radio button to choose how you want to connect to the Internet, such as dial-up access or broadband. To continue setting up your computer for Internet access, click Next. Otherwise, click Cancel, and when the Internet Properties dialog box appears again, click Cancel. Click the Close box of the Network And Internet Connection window to make it go away.

Browsing

Once you've successfully created an account with an ISP and configured Windows XP to work with your Internet account, you're ready to explore the World Wide Web with a program called Internet Explorer, also called a browser.

The World Wide Web consists of computers located all over the world that contain text and graphics to provide information as diverse as news, shopping malls, advertisements, and software that you can copy and run on your computer. Internet Explorer acts like a window that lets your computer peek at all this information stored on the World Wide Web.

Starting

To start Internet Explorer, you can use the **Start** menu. Click the Start button to display a menu. Now click **Internet Explorer**.

For another way to start Internet Explorer, click the Start button and then click **All Programs** to display a menu. Now click **Internet Explorer**.

Throughout this chapter when you see instructions that tell you to start Internet Explorer, you can choose either one of these two methods.

When the Internet Explorer window appears, you'll see a web page known as your home page. Every time you start Internet Explorer, you'll see this home page, although the exact contents may differ slightly from day to day. From this home page, you can browse the World Wide Web. (Don't worry. If you don't like your current home page, you can always change it later.)

Navigating

When you see your home page, this is Internet Explorer's way of asking, "What do you want to look at now?" To look at a different web page, you have to tell Internet Explorer which web page you want to look at. To tell Internet Explorer that you want to see a different web page, you can click a link (also called a hyperlink) that points to another web page or give Internet Explorer the address of a specific web page that you want to look at.

Clicking a Link

Nearly every web page displays links that you can click that will take you to another web page. A link acts like a button that points to a specific web page on the Internet. When you click a link, you give Internet Explorer the command to display the web page that the link points to.

Links can appear as either text or graphics. To help you locate a link, many web pages organize links as menu items along the top, left side, or bottom of a web page (see Figure 4-3). In addition, they may also highlight text links in a different color or with an underline.

Back and Forward buttons   Home button   Address box   Go button

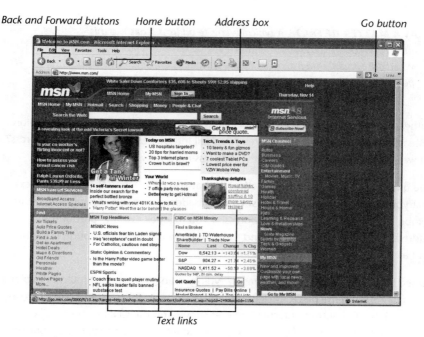

Text links

Figure 4-3 *Typical locations of links on a web page.*

Graphic links often appear as nothing more than just another picture on a web page, so graphic links typically appear next to a text link. That way, you can see the same web page whether you click the graphic link or its accompanying text link.

Although web pages try to give visual clues so that you can identify all the available links, you can use your mouse to identify a link on any web page. When you move the mouse pointer over a text or graphic link, the mouse pointer turns into a hand pointer. This is Internet Explorer's way of telling you, "Hey, you just found a link."

To see how to navigate the Internet with a click of the mouse, start Internet Explorer to display your home page. Move the mouse around your home page until the mouse pointer turns into a hand pointer. Click the mouse over the link. Internet Explorer displays a new web page for you to look at. Click the Close box of the Internet Explorer window to make it go away.

Typing an Address

While you can browse the Internet using the mouse to click web page links, links have two problems. First, you may need to click several links in succession to find a particular web page. Second, no web page will ever contain links to all the web pages on the Internet that you might want to visit.

AS A MATTER OF FACT *A typical web site address looks like this: http://www.address.com. Rather than type all this out, you can just type www.address.com and Internet Explorer automatically fills in the http:// part of the address.*

Rather than click a link, just type a specific web page address into Internet Explorer instead. When you type in an address, you tell Internet Explorer, "See this address? Show me the web page stored at that address right now."

The biggest drawback with this method is that you must know the exact address that you want to visit and you must type that address correctly despite any bizarre symbols that may be part of the address. If you misspell just one part of the address, Internet Explorer won't find the web page you want (although it might find a completely different web page instead).

To see how you can view web pages by typing in an address, start Internet Explorer to display your home page. Click in the Address box and type **www.cnn.com** and then click the Go button. Internet Explorer shows you the CNN web site. Click in the Address box again and type **www.yahoo.com** and then click the Go button. Internet Explorer shows you the Yahoo! Web site.

Click the Close box of the Internet Explorer window to make it go away.

Going Back and Forward

As you visit different web pages, you may suddenly decide that you want to view the last web page you saw again. Rather than having to type that preceding web page's address again, you can just click the Back button instead. The Back button tells Internet Explorer, "Remember that last web page I just looked at? Well, I want to see it again."

Once you click the Back button, you can then click the Forward button. When you click the Forward button, you tell Internet Explorer, "Take me to the web page that I saw after I looked at the web page that's currently displayed."

AS A MATTER OF FACT *The Back button appears dimmed until you visit a web page other than your home page. The Forward button appears dimmed until you first click the Back button.*

To see how the Back and Forward buttons work, start Internet Explorer to display your home page. Click in the Address box and type **www.foxnews.com** and then click the Go button. Internet Explorer shows you the Fox News web site. Click the

Back button. Internet Explorer shows you the last web page you looked at, which was your home page.

Click the Forward button. Internet Explorer now shows you the next web page that you saw after your home page, which was the Fox News web site. Click the Close box of the Internet Explorer window to make it go away.

Going to the Past

The Back button lets you view the last web page you saw. But if you want to view a web page that you looked at a long time ago, you don't want to click the Back button over and over again until you find a web page you once looked at. Even worse, if you want to see a web page that you visited several days ago, the Back button will show you only the previous web pages you viewed since you started Internet Explorer.

As an alternative to the Back button, you can use the Go To command that lists the past few web pages you looked at. From this list, you can just click the web page that you want to see and Internet Explorer immediately takes you back to that last-viewed web page.

To see how the Go To command works, start Internet Explorer to display your home page. Click in the Address box and type **www.yahoo.com** and then click the Go button. Internet Explorer shows you the Yahoo! web site. Click any link. Internet Explorer shows you a new web page. Click another link and Internet Explorer shows you another new web page.

Click the **View** menu and then click **Go To**. A menu pops up that displays the last few web pages you viewed. Click the name of any of these web pages. Internet Explorer shows you that web page. Click the Close box of the Internet Explorer window to make it go away.

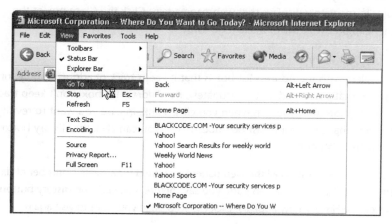

Figure 4-4 *The Go To menu lists the previous web pages you looked at.*

Visiting an Old Address

Each time you type an address into the Address box, Internet Explorer remembers that address. So when you want to go back to a web page address that you had previously typed in, you can quickly jump to that address again. Just click the Address list box, and when Internet Explorer shows you a list of all the web site addresses you once typed in, click the address you want to visit again (see Figure 4-5).

To see how to use the Address list box, start Internet Explorer to display your home page.

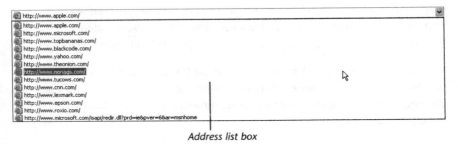

Address list box

Figure 4-5 *The Address list box remembers all previous web site addresses you typed in.*

Click in the Address box and type **www.microsoft.com** and then click the Go button. Internet Explorer shows you the Microsoft web site. Click in the Address box, type **www.apple.com**, and then click the Go button. Internet Explorer shows you the Apple Computer web site.

Click the Address list box. Internet Explorer displays a list of the previous web site addresses you typed in. Click any web site name from the Address list box. Internet Explorer immediately displays that web page again. Click the Close box of the Internet Explorer window to make it go away.

Visiting History

One problem with the Address list box is that it keeps track of addresses only for web pages that you typed in. Unfortunately, the Address list box won't keep track of any web pages that you visit when you click a link. In case you want to revisit a web page that the Address list box doesn't list, you can click the History button and view the History list.

The History list remembers all the web pages you visited for a specific number of days. When you want to revisit a web page you saw before, just click the History button, and when the History view appears, click the web page you want to visit again.

Clicking the History List   To see how the History list works, start Internet Explorer to display your home page. Click the History button. Internet Explorer shows you the History list, which organizes your previously viewed web pages by day such as Monday or Friday. Click a day to see all the web pages you visited that day. Click a web page. Internet Explorer displays your web page.

History list   History button

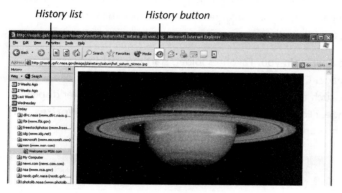

Figure 4-6
The History list shows you every web page you visited in the past few days.

Click the Close box of the History list pane and then click the Close box of the Internet Explorer window to make it go away.

Setting a Time Limit   The History list remembers every web page you visited up to a certain number of days, such as 20. To increase or decrease this time limit, start Internet Explorer to display your home page. Click the **Tools** menu and then click **Internet Options**. When the Internet Options dialog box appears, click the up or down arrow of the Days To Keep Pages In History text box (see Figure 4-7). If you click Clear History, you can clear the entire History list.

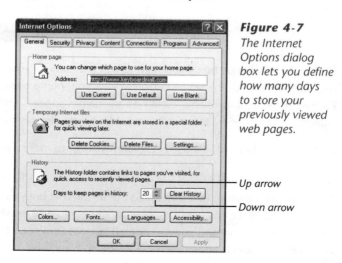

Figure 4-7
The Internet Options dialog box lets you define how many days to store your previously viewed web pages.

Up arrow

Down arrow

Click OK and then click the Close box of the Internet Explorer window to make it go away.

Favorites

Rather than memorize the addresses of your favorite web pages, you can store them in a special Favorites folder. That way, when you want to visit a certain web page again, you can just look in your Favorites folder and click the name of the web page you want to visit again.

To store a web page address in your Favorites folder, start Internet Explorer to display your home page. Click in the Address box and type the address of a web page you visit often, such as **www.google.com**. When Internet Explorer displays your chosen web page, click the **Favorites** menu and click **Add To Favorites**. An Add Favorite dialog box appears.

Figure 4-8
The Add Favorite dialog box can store addresses for all your favorite web sites.

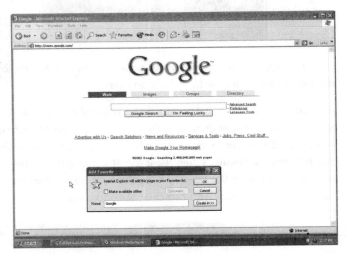

Click in the Name text box if you want to edit the name of your favorite web page. Click OK. Click the Home button to view your home page. Now click the **Favorites** menu, and when a list of web site names appears, click the web site name you want to view. Internet Explorer obediently displays your chosen web site.

Click the Close box of the Internet Explorer window to make it go away.

Searching

Sometimes you want to find something on the Internet but you don't quite know where to look. Since you won't know what address to type or which links to click to get you what you want, you can just tell Internet Explorer, "This is the topic I'm interested in. Now go out on the World Wide Web and find me a list of all web sites that might have the information I want."

To see how you can search the World Wide Web, start Internet Explorer to display your home page. Click the Search button. A Search Companion panel pops up on the left side of the Internet Explorer window. Click in the Query text box and type a word or phrase of the topic you want to view, such as scuba diving or Apple Computers. Click the Search button.

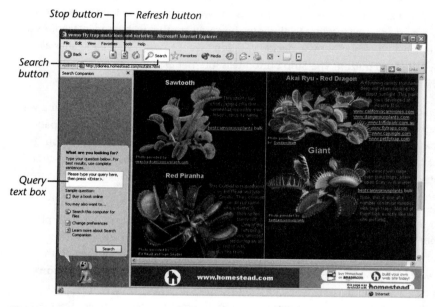

Figure 4-9 *With the Search Companion, you can look for information on the World Wide Web.*

The Search Companion and the Internet Explorer window display a list of links related to the word or phrase you typed. Click the Close box of the Search Companion and then click the Close box of the Internet Explorer window to make it go away.

Going Home

Your home page appears every time you start Internet Explorer. At any time, you can return to your home page if you click the Home button. To see how the Home button works, start Internet Explorer to display your home page.

Click in the Address text box and type a web site address, such as **www.amazon.com**, and then click the Go button. Now click the Home button. Internet Explorer brings you back to your home page. Click the Close box of the Internet Explorer window to make it go away.

In case you want to change your home page, start Internet Explorer to display your home page. Click the **Tools** menu and click **Internet Options**. The Internet

Options dialog box appears. Click in the Address text box and type the address of a new web page, such as **www.tucows.com**, and click OK. Click the Close box of the Internet Explorer window to make it go away.

Stopping and Refreshing

If you decide to view a web page and suddenly change your mind, you normally have to wait until Internet Explorer loads the web page you no longer want to see before you can tell Internet Explorer to show you another web page instead. As an alternative, the moment you decide you don't want to see a web page after all, click the Stop button. The Stop button tells Internet Explorer, "Stop doing whatever you're doing so I can give you another command to do right now."

Similar to the Stop button is the Refresh button. Sometimes you may look at a web page that contains information that changes fairly regularly, such as a web page listing stock prices or sports scores. To make sure Internet Explorer shows you the latest data on a web page, click the Refresh button. The Refresh button tells Internet Explorer, "Reload the web page currently displayed so I can see the latest version of this web page."

To see how the Stop and Refresh buttons work, start Internet Explorer to display your home page. Click in the Address box, type **www.bbc.co.uk**, click the Go button, and then click the Stop button. Internet Explorer stops loading the **www.bbc.co.uk** web site. Click in the Address list box, type **www.nyse.com**, and click the Go button. When Internet Explorer displays the New York Stock Exchange web site, click the Refresh button. Internet Explorer removes the New York Stock Exchange web page from view and then displays it again. Depending on the time and day you do this, you may be able to notice that the data on the web page changed after you clicked the Refresh button.

Click the Close box of the Internet Explorer window to make it go away.

Saving

As you browse through different web pages, you may want to save one to show to others or to keep for reference. To save a web page, you can either store a copy of it (including graphics) on your disk or you can print a copy on paper.

Saving a Web Page

When you save a web page, Internet Explorer saves that web page along with all the graphics on that web page. When you want to view a saved web page, just start Internet Explorer and load your saved web page.

To see how you can save a web page and view it again, start Internet Explorer to display your home page. Click in the Address box and type **www.theonion.com** and click the Go button. Click the **File** menu and click **Save As**. A Save As dialog box appears. Click the My Documents button that appears on the left side of the Save As dialog box and click Save.

Click the Home button to view your home page. Now click the **File** menu and then click **Open**. An Open dialog box appears. Click Browse. Another dialog box appears that looks identical to the Save As dialog box you saw earlier.

Click the My Documents icon on the left side of the dialog box, click the web page name you want to view, and then click Open. Internet Explorer shows your saved web page. Click the Close box of the Internet Explorer window to make it go away.

AS A MATTER OF FACT *When you view a saved web page, the contents never change, unlike viewing a web page off the Internet.*

Printing a Web Page

As an alternative to or instead of saving a web page to your disk, you can print it out instead. To see how to print a web page, start Internet Explorer to display your home page. Click in the Address box and type **www.reuters.com** and click the Go button. Click the **File** menu and click **Print**. A Print dialog box appears. Turn on your printer and then click Print.

Click the Close box of the Internet Explorer window to make it go away.

Handling E-Mail

While Internet Explorer lets you view web pages from computers around the world, Outlook Express lets you send and receive e-mail from people around the world. Although most people use e-mail to send and receive messages, you can also use e-mail to exchange pictures and even programs with others.

Starting Outlook Express

When you want to send or receive e-mail, you need to start Outlook Express. To start Outlook Express, click the Start button and click **Outlook Express**.

If the Internet Explorer window already appears, you can either click the Mail button or click the **Tools** menu, click **Mail And News**, and then click **Read Mail** to start Outlook Express.

When you see instructions that tell you to start Outlook Express, you can choose either of the preceding methods to display the Outlook Express window.

Creating an Account

Before you can send or receive e-mail, you need to tell Outlook Express how to work with your e-mail account, which consists of four crucial bits of information: your ID or account name, your password, the name of your incoming mail server, and the name of your outgoing mail server.

When you sign up with an ISP, you must choose an ID or account name. This name forms part of your e-mail address, so if you choose an ID such as BigLoser and you sign up with the Microsoft Network, your complete e-mail address would be BigLoser@msn.com.

To make sure that only you have access to your e-mail account, your ISP will ask that you choose a password. To access your e-mail account, Outlook Express needs to know your ID and your password.

When someone sends e-mail to you, they don't send it directly to your computer. Instead, they send it to your ISP's computer, known as a server. Then the ISP server forwards your e-mail directly to your computer.

So when you tell Outlook Express that you want to receive e-mail, the first thing that Outlook Express needs to know is the name of your incoming mail server. Once Outlook Express knows the name of this incoming mail server, it can find this server on the Internet whenever you want to retrieve your e-mail.

When you want to send e-mail to someone else, you don't send e-mail directly to that person's computer. Instead, you send your e-mail to your ISP's server and this server forwards this e-mail on to your recipient. So when you want to send e-mail, you have to tell Outlook Express the name of your outgoing mail server.

AS A MATTER OF FACT *You must get your ID (account name), password, incoming mail server, and outgoing mail server name from your ISP. Without this information, you won't be able to send or receive e-mail with Outlook Express.*

To tell Outlook Express how to work with your e-mail account, start Outlook Express. Click the **Tools** menu and click **Accounts**. An Internet Accounts dialog box appears. Click the Mail tab, click the Add button, and when a menu appears, click Mail. An Internet Connection Wizard dialog box appears that asks how you want your name to appear in any e-mail messages you send.

Type your name and click Next. Another Internet Connection Wizard dialog box appears that asks your e-mail address. Type your complete e-mail address, which is the combination of your ID or account name plus the name of your ISP, such as luzer@aol.com or billgates@msn.com. Click Next.

Another Internet Connection Wizard dialog box appears that asks you the name of your incoming and outgoing mail servers. Type this information in the Incoming Mail Server and Outgoing Mail Server text boxes and then click Next. Another Internet Connection Wizard dialog box appears that asks for your account name and password. Type this information in the Account Name and Password text boxes and click Next.

A final Internet Connection Wizard dialog box appears to inform you that you are finished setting up your e-mail account. Click Finish. The Internet Accounts dialog box now displays your newly created e-mail account in the Mail tab portion of the dialog box. Click Close and then click the Close box of the Outlook Express window to make it go away.

Writing

From your computer's point of view, the most important part when you send e-mail is that you type the recipient's e-mail address correctly. Misspell the e-mail address and your e-mail will never arrive at its destination.

Sending

To write an e-mail message, start Outlook Express. Click the Create Mail button. A New Message dialog box appears. Click in the To: text box and type the e-mail address of the person you want to receive your message (see Figure 4-10). Click in the Subject text box and type the subject of your message. Now click in the Message text box and type your message.

When you're done, click the Send button. Click the Close box of the Outlook Express window to make it go away.

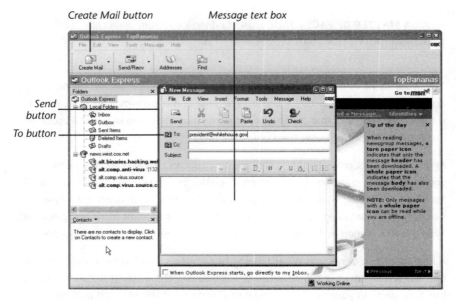

Create Mail button   Message text box

Send button

To button

Figure 4-10 *When you write a message, you must specify the e-mail address of the recipient.*

Attaching a File

In addition to sending text, you can also send files such as word processor documents, pictures, or music files. To see how to attach a file to your e-mail message, start Outlook Express. Click the Create Mail button. A New Message dialog box appears.

Click the Insert menu and then click File Attachment. An Insert Attachment dialog box appears. Click the file you want to attach to your e-mail message and then click Attach. The New Message window displays the name and icon of your attached file.

At this point, you can type an e-mail address in the To: text box, type a subject in the Subject text box, and then click the Send button to send your message and attached file to another person.

Reading

Once you've set up your e-mail account, you can give out your e-mail address and receive e-mail from others. Outlook Express checks for new e-mail periodically, and when it finds e-mail waiting for you, it retrieves that e-mail so that you can read it at your leisure.

Retrieving E-Mail

To read e-mail in Outlook Express, start Outlook Express. Click the Inbox folder in the Folders list. Outlook Express displays a list of e-mail messages in the Message list where any new e-mail messages appear in bold (see Figure 4-11). Click the e-mail message that you want to read. Outlook Express displays the contents of your chosen message in the Preview pane. (If the message is too big to fit into the Preview pane, you can click the up or down arrows of the preview pane scroll bar to scroll through the message.)

Click the Close box of the Outlook Express window to make it go away.

Figure 4-11 *Outlook Express highlights new messages in bold.*

Responding to E-Mail

Many times when you read an e-mail message, you may want to write a response back right away. When you respond to an e-mail message, your new e-mail message contains the text of the message that you're responding to.

To respond to an e-mail message, start Outlook Express and then click the Inbox folder in the Folders list. Outlook Express displays a list of e-mail messages in the Message list, where any new e-mail messages appear in bold. Click the e-mail message that you want to respond to and then click the Reply button. Outlook

Express displays a New Message window, which contains the text of the message you're responding to.

Click in the Message text box and type your message. When you're done, click the Send button. Notice that when you respond to a message, you don't need to type an e-mail address or a subject, since Outlook Express includes this information automatically.

Click the Close box of the Outlook Express window to make it go away.

Saving a File Attachment

When someone sends you a file attached to a message, Outlook Express displays a paper clip icon next to that message. To save an attached file, open the Outlook Express window and then click the message that contains the paper clip icon. Outlook Express displays your message in the Preview pane along with a larger paper clip icon. At this point, you can either save the file (so that you can open it later) or open it right away.

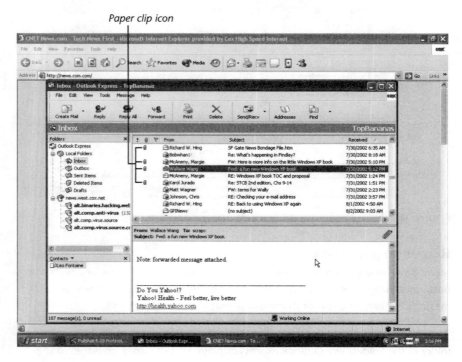

Paper clip icon

Figure 4-12 *A paper clip icon identifies all messages that have an attached file.*

To save an attached file, click the paper clip icon in the upper right-hand corner of the Preview pane. A pull-down menu appears that lists all the files attached to the message.

Click **Save Attachments**. A Save Attachments dialog box appears. Click Browse to switch to a different drive or folder and then click OK. Then click Save.

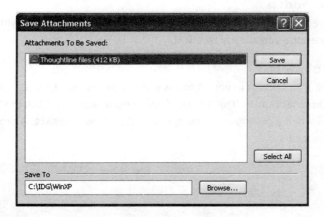

Figure 4-13   You can save an attached file on any disk in your computer.

If you want to view an attached file, click the paper clip icon in the upper right-hand corner of the Preview pane. A pull-down menu appears that lists all the files attached to the message.

Click the name of the attached file. An Open Attachment Warning dialog box appears. Click the Open It radio button and then click OK. As long as you have a program that can open the attached file, that program automatically loads and displays the contents of the attached file.

Using the Address Book

As you start to send and receive e-mail regularly, you may find that you tend to send e-mail to the same people. Rather than try to memorize all the e-mail addresses of everyone you write to, you can store those addresses in the Outlook Express Address Book instead.

The next time you write an e-mail message, you don't have to type in that person's e-mail address. Just click that person's name stored in your Address Book and Outlook Express types that person's e-mail address in automatically.

Saving an Address

You can save an address by typing it into your Address Book or by copying it from an e-mail message you already received.

Typing an Address

To type an e-mail address in your Address Book, start Outlook Express and then click the Addresses button. The Address Book window appears. Click the New button, and when a pull-down menu appears, click **New Contact**. A properties dialog box appears.

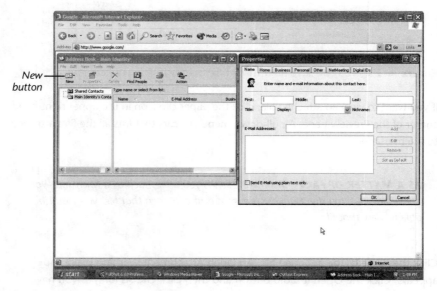

Figure 4-14 *You can store a person's name and e-mail address in the Outlook Express Address Book.*

Click in the First, Middle, and Last text boxes and type a person's first, middle, and last name. Click in the E-Mail Addresses text box and type that person's e-mail address and then click OK. Click the Close box of the Outlook Express window to make it go away.

Copying an Address

To copy an e-mail address into the Address Book from an existing e-mail message, start Outlook Express.

Click the Inbox icon in the Folders list. Outlook Express displays a list of stored e-mail messages in the Messages pane. Right-click a message in the Messages pane, and when a pop-up menu appears, click **Add Sender To Address Book**. Your chosen e-mail address and person's name immediately appears in the Contacts list.

Click the Close box of the Outlook Express window to make it go away.

Retrieving an Address

After you save an e-mail address in your Address Book, you can retrieve that e-mail address when you want to send that person a message. To retrieve an e-mail address, start Outlook Express.

Click the Create Mail button. A New Message window appears. Click the To: button. A Select Recipients dialog box appears. Click the name you want to use and then click the To:-> button. Your chosen e-mail address appears in the Message Recipients text box. Click OK. At this point, you can type in the Message text box and then click the Send button.

Click the Close box of the Outlook Express window to make it go away.

Deleting an Address

After a while, you may have e-mail addresses stored in your Address Book that you no longer want. To delete an address, start Outlook Express.

Right-click the name you want to delete in the Contacts list. When a pop-up menu appears, click **Delete**. When a dialog box appears and asks if you really want to delete the e-mail address, click Yes. Click the Close box of the Outlook Express window to make it go away.

Reading Newsgroups

Newsgroups act like the Internet equivalent of a cork bulletin board where anyone can post a message that others can read and respond to with a message of their own. A newsgroup typically focuses on a specific topic, such as model trains or bird watching.

Unlike e-mail that's usually sent to a single person, newsgroups contain messages that anyone can read. Newsgroups simply allow people interested in similar topics to share ideas in a public forum.

Configuring Outlook Express

To read a newsgroup, you must first tell Outlook Express the name of your ISP's news server computer. To define your news server computer name, start Outlook Express.

Click the **Tools** menu and then click **Accounts**. An Internet Accounts dialog box appears. Click the News tab and then click Add. When a menu appears, click News.

An Internet Connection Wizard dialog box appears. Click in the Display Name text box and type a name that you want others to see when you post a message in a newsgroup. This name does not have to be your real name. Then click Next.

Click in the E-Mail Address text box and type an e-mail address that you want others to use to contact you. Then click Next. Click in the News (NNTP) Server text box and type the name of your ISP's news server. You must get this information from your ISP. Click Next and then click Finish.

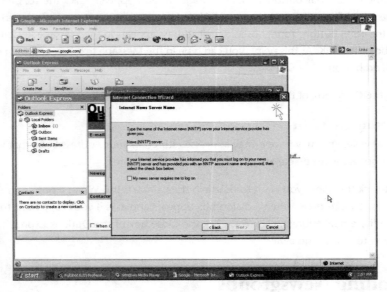

Figure 4-15 *Before you can read newsgroups, you must create a news account in Outlook Express.*

The Internet Accounts dialog box appears again. Click Close. A dialog box appears that asks if you want to download a list of newsgroups. Click Yes.

Finding a Newsgroup

Once you've told Outlook Express the name of your ISP's news server, you can browse through the thousands of newsgroups available on the Internet. Since it's unlikely that you'll want to read messages in every newsgroup available, you need to tell Outlook Express which newsgroups you want to view or subscribe to.

> **AS A MATTER OF FACT**   When you subscribe to a newsgroup, it won't cost you a thing.

Subscribing

To subscribe to a newsgroup, start Outlook Express. Click the **Tools** menu and click **Newsgroups**. A Newsgroup Subscriptions dialog box appears.

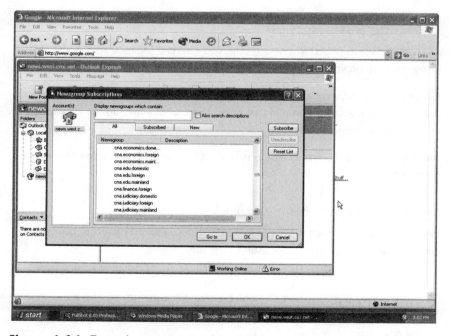

Figure 4-16   To read messages stored in a newsgroup, you must subscribe to that newsgroup first.

Click in the Display Newsgroups Which Contain text box and type a word that describes the topic of the newsgroup you want to examine, such as fish or virus. As you type, the Newsgroup Subscriptions dialog box displays a list of newsgroups that contain the word you typed. Click a newsgroup name and click Subscribe. Repeat these steps for each newsgroup that you want to view.

Click OK. Outlook Express displays all your subscribed newsgroups in the Folders list. Click the Close box of the Outlook Express window.

Unsubscribing

Once you subscribe to a newsgroup, you may find that you don't want to read its messages after all. To unsubscribe from a newsgroup, start Outlook Express. Click the **Tools** menu and click **Newsgroups**. A Newsgroup Subscriptions dialog box appears. Click the Subscribe tab. Outlook Express shows you a list of all the newsgroups you have subscribed to.

Click a newsgroup that you don't want to view any more and then click Unsubscribe. Click OK. Click the Close box of the Outlook Express window.

Browsing a Newsgroup

After you have subscribed to a newsgroup, you can read the messages stored in that newsgroup. To browse through a newsgroup's messages, start Outlook Express.

Click the newsgroup name in the Folders list. The Messages pane of Outlook Express displays all the messages stored in that newsgroup. Click a message to view its contents in the Preview pane.

When you're done, click the Close box of the Outlook Express window to make it go away.

Posting a Message

While you could just read messages in a newsgroup, you may want to post your own message or respond to an existing message.

Creating a New Message

To create a new message, start Outlook Express. Click the newsgroup name in the Folders list. The Messages pane of Outlook Express displays all the messages stored in that newsgroup (see Figure 4-17).

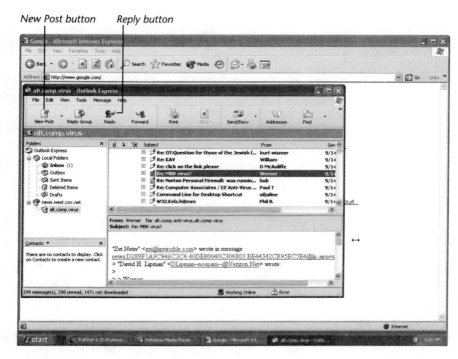

New Post button   *Reply button*

Figure 4-17 *Outlook Express can display messages stored in a newsgroup.*

Click the New Post button. A New Message window appears. Click in the Subject text box and type a subject. Then, click in the Message text box and type your message. Finally, click the Send button.

When you're done, click the Close box of the Outlook Express window to make it go away.

Responding to a Message

To respond to an existing message, first start Outlook Express.

Click the newsgroup name in the Folders list. The Messages pane of Outlook Express displays all the messages stored in that newsgroup. Click a message to view its contents in the Preview pane.

Click the Reply button. Type your text in the Message text box and then click the Send button. When you're done, click the Close box of the Outlook Express window to make it go away.

Figure 4-37   [illegible caption text]

Click the New tool in tool palette. Notice in bottom of screen [illegible] scroll bar and vertical scroll [illegible]. [illegible] OK. The [illegible] button [illegible] properties dialog. Click the Apply [illegible]

When you're done with the dialog box [illegible], choose [illegible] to make it GO AWAY.

Scrolling in Stages

2. [illegible] to affect a number of items at once instead of one at a time.

Click the [illegible] tool in the tool palette. Look at the lower left corner of the screen. [illegible] will now appear in the view, using it [illegible] place [illegible] around the element you want to remain visible.

Out on [illegible] the [illegible] part in the [illegible] video [illegible] appear in a [illegible] scroll button, which gives the element [illegible] center the button to [illegible] area.

5

Working with Windows XP

Windows XP comes with several programs, including a word processor (WordPad), a paint program (Microsoft Paint), some games (Solitaire and Minesweeper), a web browser (Internet Explorer), an e-mail program (Outlook Express), and some handy utilities, such as a calculator. While these programs can come in handy at times, you will probably want to run other types of programs on your computer.

If you can think of a specific use for your computer, chances are good that someone has written a program that can do what you want, whether you want to manage rental property, write a screenplay, edit digital video, pick lottery numbers, or play a video game.

Once you buy a program that you need, you need to install it on your own computer and then once it's installed, you need to know how to load the program so you can use it. Sometimes you may find that you don't use a particular program so rather than let it gobble up space, you can remove or uninstall it from your computer at any time. By knowing how to load, install, and remove programs, you can customize your computer and Windows XP to perform nearly any task.

Installation

Before you can run a program on your computer, you have to install it. When you install a program, Windows XP includes that program's name and icon in the All Programs menu that appears when you click the Start button. The two most common ways to install a program are from a CD or through the Internet.

AS A MATTER OF FACT *If you just copy a program to your computer like an ordinary file, Windows XP won't list that program's name on the All Programs menu and the program may not run properly.*

Installing from a CD

Most programs that you can buy from the store come stored on a CD. To install a program off the CD, you usually just have to insert the CD in your CD drive for the installation program to start up automatically. Once the installation program appears, just follow the directions to install the program on your computer.

Figure 5-1
An installation program that often runs automatically when you insert the CD in your computer.

Installing from the Internet

You may also want to install programs that you find on the Internet. Programs offered over the Internet usually come stored in a special installation program so that you just have to copy this one file to your computer. Once you've copied this installation program on your computer, you can run it. From this point on, you just need to follow the onscreen instructions to install the program on your computer.

When you copy a program from the Internet, Windows XP displays a dialog box that asks if you want to Open or Save the program. If you choose Open, Windows XP starts to install that program on your computer. If you choose Save, Windows XP saves the installation program on your computer so that you can run it at a later time.

Figure 5-2
When you copy a program off the Internet, you can either Open or Save it.

Running a Program

Once you've successfully installed a program on your computer, you can run it. Windows XP provides several ways to run a program, so you can choose the method that you like the best.

Clicking the All Programs Menu

When you click the Start button, you can click **All Programs** to view a list of every program installed on your computer. If you have many programs installed, this list can get cluttered, which can make finding the program you want somewhat difficult.

To see how to run a program from the **All Programs** menu, click the Start button and then click **All Programs**. A list of every program installed on your computer appears (see Figure 5-3).

Figure 5-3
*The All Programs
menu displays
program groups
and program
names.*

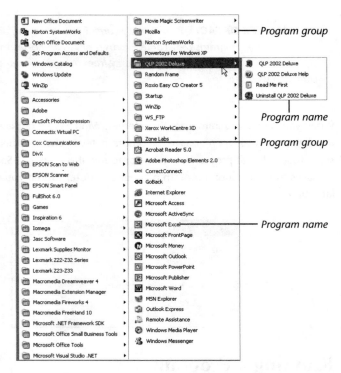

If a name on the **All Programs** menu does not appear with a little arrow pointing
to the right, then that name represents a program. If you click that program name,
you can run the program right away.

If a name appears on the **All Programs** menu with a little arrow pointing to the right,
then that name represents a program group. When you move or click the mouse
pointer over a program group, another menu appears. This additional menu always
displays a program name but may also display a help file, an uninstallation program,
or a ReadMe file that contains additional instructions for using the program. To run a
program that appears in this additional menu, just click the program name.

Click anywhere away from the **Start** menu or **All Programs** list to make them
go away.

Clicking a Desktop Icon

Many people find the **All Programs** menu clumsy to use, so Windows XP offers
desktop icons as a shortcut. A desktop icon displays a program's icon directly on
the Windows XP desktop. So the next time you want to run that program, you can
skip the All Programs menu and just double-click the desktop icon instead.

When you install some programs, they automatically put a program icon on your desktop, but if your favorite program does not, you can put the icons of your favorite programs on your desktop manually.

To see how to use desktop icons, click the Start button and then click **All Programs**. The **All Programs** menu appears.

Click **Accessories** and then right-click **Paint**. A pop-up menu appears. Click **Send To**. Another menu appears. Click **Desktop (Create shortcut)**. Windows XP puts the Paint icon on your desktop.

Double-click the Paint desktop icon. Windows XP loads the Microsoft Paint program in its own window. Click the close box of the Paint window to make it go away.

Clicking the Start Menu

Putting icons of your most frequently used programs on the desktop can give you fast access to your programs. Unfortunately, you may find that too many icons can clutter up your desktop. As an alternative, you can store the icons of your favorite programs directly on the **Start** menu instead. That way, everytime you click the Start button, you can see your most frequently used programs directly on the **Start** menu.

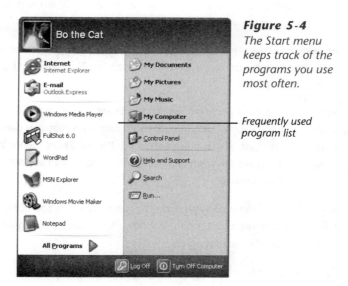

Figure 5-4
The Start menu keeps track of the programs you use most often.

Frequently used program list

Windows XP gives you two ways to display program icons directly on the **Start** menu. You can drag a program icon to the top of the **Start** menu, or if you use a program often enough, Windows XP automatically stores that program's icon in the bottom of the **Start** menu.

Dragging an Icon

To put a program on the **Start** menu, click the Start button and then click **All Programs**. The **All Programs** menu appears. Click **Accessories** and then move the mouse pointer over **Calculator**.

Drag the Calculator icon to the top of the **Start** menu. A plus sign appears near the bottom of the mouse pointer, and a black horizontal line appears. Release the left mouse button. Windows XP displays the Calculator icon in the top half of the **Start** menu. Click the Calculator icon in the **Start** menu. The Calculator window appears. Click the close box of the Calculator window to make it go away.

Pinning an Icon

When you've loaded a certain program often enough, Windows XP displays that program's icon in the bottom of the **Start** menu. Your most frequently used program icons appear in the top of the frequently used program list, while your less frequently used programs appear near the bottom.

If a program icon appears on this list of frequently used programs but you don't use that particular program after a while, Windows XP automatically removes that program's icon from the **Start** menu.

In case you see a program icon that you always want to keep on the **Start** menu, you can pin that icon to the frequently used list. That way, that particular program icon always appears.

To see how to pin a program icon to the **Start** menu, click the Start button. A menu appears. Right-click over any program icon that you want to pin to the frequently used list. A menu appears. Click **Pin to Start** menu. Windows XP moves your pinned program icon out of the frequently used list and up to the top of the **Start** menu.

Right-click that same program icon that appears at the top of the **Start** menu. Click **Unpin from Start** menu. Windows XP moves the program icon back down to the frequently used list again.

Increasing/Decreasing the Frequently Used List

Windows XP normally displays six program icons in the frequently used list on the **Start** menu. However, you can increase or decrease this number.

To change the number of program icons that appear in the frequently used list, right-click the Start button and when a menu appears, click **Properties**. A Taskbar and Start Menu Properties dialog box appears.

Figure 5-5 *You can edit the frequently used list on the Start menu.*

Click Customize. Click the up or down arrow of the Number of programs on the **Start** menu text box. Click OK. The Taskbar and Start Menu Properties dialog box appears again. Click OK.

Click the Start button. Notice that the frequently used list on the **Start** menu has changed to reflect the number you chose. Press **ESC** to make the **Start** menu disappear.

Clicking Quick Launch

Since it's faster to click an icon than to wade through the **Start** and **All Programs** menus to find the program you want to run, Windows XP offers yet another way to click a program icon to run a program quickly: Quick Launch.

The Quick Launch toolbar displays program icons directly on the taskbar to the right of the Start button. To save space on the taskbar, Windows XP normally hides the Quick Launch toolbar from view, but you may want to sacrifice space on the taskbar to display Quick Launch toolbar.

To view and place an icon on the Quick Launch toolbar, right-click a blank part of the taskbar. When a menu pops up, click **Toolbars** and then click **Quick Launch**.

Windows XP displays the Quick Launch toolbar, which already contains icons for Internet Explorer and Outlook Express.

Quick Launch buttons

Figure 5-6 *The Quick Launch toolbar lets you run your favorite programs quickly.*

Click the Start button and click **All Programs**. Click **Accessories** and then move the mouse pointer over to **Calculator**. Drag the mouse over the Quick Launch icons until you see a black vertical line appear. Then release the left mouse button. Windows XP puts the Calculator icon on Quick Launch.

Click the Calculator icon on Quick Launch. The Calculator window appears. Click the close box of the Calculator window to make it go away.

Right-click the Calculator icon on Quick Launch. A menu appears. Click **Delete**. A dialog box appears that asks if you are sure you want to delete the Calculator icon. Click Yes.

To hide Quick Launch, right-click a blank part of the taskbar. When a menu appears, click **Toolbars** and then **Quick Launch**. Windows XP hides Quick Launch from the taskbar.

Clicking the Desktop Toolbar

One problem with storing program icons on the desktop is that when you load one or more programs, those program windows cover up your desktop icons. To give you quick access to all your desktop icons, you can also display your desktop icons in a **Desktop** toolbar on the taskbar.

Normally Windows XP hides this **Desktop** menu to save space on the taskbar, but to make this **Desktop** toolbar visible, right-click a blank spot on the taskbar. When a menu appears, click **Toolbars** and then click **Desktop**. Windows XP displays the **Desktop** toolbar near the right side of the taskbar.

Desktop toolbar

Double-pointing arrow button

Figure 5-7 *The Desktop toolbar displays all your desktop icons in a convenient menu.*

Click the double-pointing arrow button to the right of the Desktop toolbar. A menu appears that displays all your desktop icons.

To hide the Desktop toolbar, right-click a blank spot on the taskbar and when a menu appears, click **Toolbars** and then click **Desktop**. The Desktop toolbar disappears from the taskbar.

Using the Run Command

If you download a program from the Internet or if you insert a program on a CD or floppy disk in your computer, the **Start** menu won't know that this program exists. When you want to run a program that doesn't appear as a desktop or Quick Launch icon or in the **Start** menu, you can use the Run command.

When you use the Run command, you must tell Windows XP the location of the program you want to run. To see how the Run command works, click the Start button and click **Run**. A Run dialog box appears.

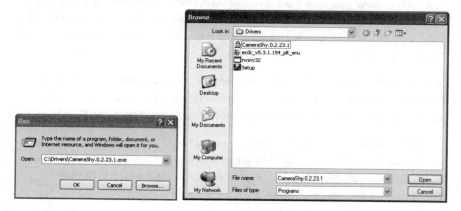

Figure 5-8 *The Run command lets you choose a specific file to load.*

Click Browse. A Browse dialog box appears. Click the Windows folder in the Open dialog box and click Open. Click Notepad and click Open.

The Run dialog box displays the drive, folder name, and filename of the Notepad program. Click OK. The Notepad window appears. Click the close box of the Notepad window to make it go away.

Loading Your Document

One problem with loading programs is that you often have to go through a two-step process to start working on your previously saved data. First you have to load the program that you want to use. Second, you have to load the file that contains the data you want to use.

To simplify this process, you can load your data and your program at the same time through either the Windows Explorer or a desktop icon that represents your data.

Using Windows Explorer

You can use the Windows Explorer to find any file on your computer (see Chapter 3 for more details). Once you've found the file you want to use, just double-click that file and Windows XP automatically loads that file along with the program that created it.

To see how to load a document and a program at the same time, click the Start button and click **All Programs**. Click **Accessories** and then click **WordPad**. The WordPad window appears.

Type **This is how you can load a document and a program at the same time.** Click the **File** menu and then click **Save**. A Save As dialog box appears. Click in the file name text box, type **LoadMe**, and then click Save. Click the close box of the WordPad window.

Click the Start button and click **All Programs**. Click **Accessories** and then click **Windows Explorer**. The Windows Explorer window appears. Click the Search button and then click Documents (word processing, spreadsheet, etc.).

Click in the All or part of the document name text box, type **LoadMe**, and click Search. When Windows Explorer displays your document icon in the right side of the window, double-click that icon. The WordPad window appears with the LoadMe document already displayed.

Click the close box of the WordPad window to make it go away. Click the close box of the Windows Explorer window to make it go away.

Using a Desktop Icon

As a faster way to load a document and a program at the same time, you can put an icon on your desktop that represents your file. Then you just have to double-click this desktop icon to load your data and program at the same time.

To see how to put a document on your desktop as an icon, click the Start button and click **All Programs**. Click **Accessories** and then click **Windows Explorer**. The Windows Explorer window appears. Click the Search button and then click Documents (word processing, spreadsheet, etc.).

Click in the All or part of the document name text box, type **LoadMe**, and click Search. When Windows Explorer displays your document icon in the right side of the window, right-click that icon. A menu appears.

Click **Send To** and then **Desktop (Create shortcut)**. Click the close box of the Windows Explorer window to make it go away. Notice that Windows XP displays the document as a Shortcut to LoadMe desktop icon.

Double-click this Shortcut to LoadMe desktop icon. Windows XP loads the WordPad window with the LoadMe data already displayed inside. Click the close box of the WordPad window to make it go away.

Organizing Your Windows

Every time you load a program, Windows XP displays that program in its own separate window. Since you can run several programs at the same time, you may have two or more windows appear on your screen at once. Since this may look confusing, you need to learn all the different ways to manage your windows so that you can see what you're doing.

Switching Windows

Every time you run a program, Windows XP displays that program name as a button on the taskbar. The more programs you load, the smaller each program's button appears.

Each button on the taskbar not only shows you what programs you have loaded but also gives you quick access to that program. Any time you want to switch to another program that you have already loaded, just look for that program's button on the taskbar and then click that button.

To see how you can switch between two different program windows, click the Start button and then click **All Programs**. Click **Accessories** and then click **Calculator**. Windows XP displays the Calculator window on the screen and also displays the Calculator button on the taskbar.

Click the Start button and then click **All Programs**. Click **Accessories** and then click **WordPad**. Windows XP displays the WordPad window on the screen and also displays the WordPad button on the taskbar (see Figure 5-9).

> **AS A MATTER OF FACT** *If a program window is partially visible on the desktop, you can also switch to that program if you click the visible part of that program window.*

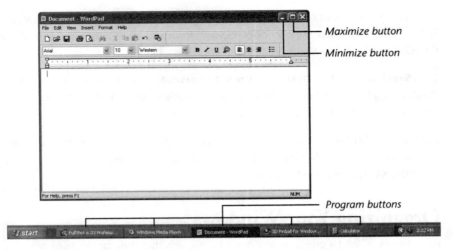

Figure 5-9 *Every program can appear in a window on the desktop and as a button on the taskbar.*

Click the Calculator button on the taskbar. The Calculator window appears. Click the WordPad button on the taskbar. Now the WordPad window appears. Click the close box of the WordPad window. Then click the close box of the Calculator window.

Minimizing a Window

If you have too many windows on the screen at once, you can *minimize* some windows. When you minimize a window, you tell Windows XP, "See that window cluttering up my screen? Make that window go away, but don't get rid of that window completely, since I might need it again." A minimized window appears only as a button on the taskbar.

Windows XP provides two ways to minimize a window. One, you can click the program button on the taskbar. Two, you can click the Minimize button in the program window.

To see how to minimize a window, click the Start button and then click **All Programs**. Click **Accessories** and then click **Paint**. Windows XP displays the Paint window on the screen and also displays the Paint button on the taskbar.

Click the Paint button on the taskbar. The Paint window pops up again. Click the Minimize button on the Paint window. The Paint window disappears again, although the Paint button still appears on the taskbar.

Click the Paint button on the taskbar. Then click the close box of the Paint window to make it go away.

Viewing the Desktop

Sometimes you may have one or more program windows on your screen, but you want to see the desktop so that you can click a desktop icon to load another program. Rather than minimize each window individually, you can minimize all the windows on your desktop at once. To see how to do this, click the Start button and then click **All Programs**. Click **Accessories** and then click **Calculator**. Windows XP displays the Calculator window on the screen.

Click the Start button and then click **All Programs**. Click **Accessories** and then click **WordPad**. Windows XP displays the WordPad window on the screen.

Right-click any blank spot on the taskbar. A menu pops up. Click **Show the Desktop**. The desktop appears right away because Windows XP automatically minimizes every program currently running.

Right-click any blank spot on the taskbar again. A menu pops up. Click **Show Open Windows**. Click the WordPad button on the taskbar and then click the close box of the WordPad window. Click the Calculator button on the taskbar and then click the close box of the Calculator window.

Maximizing a Window

While you use one program, you may not want to see all the other program windows cluttering up your screen. To hide these other program windows from view and to make the program window that you're working in as large as possible, you can *maximize* a window.

A maximized window fills the entire screen. To see how to maximize a window, click the Start button and then click **All Programs**. Click **Accessories** and then click **WordPad**. Windows XP displays the WordPad window on the screen.

Click the Maximize button on the WordPad window. The WordPad window fills the entire screen. Click the Restore button so that the WordPad window covers only part of the screen. Notice that when a window appears maximized, the Restore button appears, but when a window only covers part of the screen, the Maximize button appears. Click the close box of the WordPad window to make it go away.

Resizing

Rather than minimize or maximize a window, you can also *resize* a window. That way, if you don't want your window to fill the entire screen, you can adjust its size to your liking.

To see how to resize a window, click the Start button and then click **All Programs**. Click **Accessories** and then click **WordPad**. Windows XP displays the WordPad window on the screen.

> **AS A MATTER OF FACT** If the WordPad window appears maximized, click the Restore button. If a window is maximized, you won't be able to resize it until you click the Restore button of that window.

Move the mouse pointer over the left edge of the WordPad window. Notice that the mouse pointer turns into a double-pointing arrow. Drag the mouse to the right and left. The WordPad window shrinks and expands in the direction that you move the mouse.

Click the close box of the WordPad window to make it go away.

Moving

If a window is not minimized or maximized, you can *move* it around the screen. That way, you can open and move several windows on the screen to different locations so that you can see them at the same time.

To see how to move a window, click the Start button and then click **All Programs**. Click **Accessories** and then click **WordPad**. Windows XP displays the WordPad window on the screen.

Move the mouse pointer over title bar (top edge) of the WordPad window. Drag the mouse around the screen. The WordPad window moves in the direction that you move the mouse.

Click the close box of the WordPad window to make it go away.

Tiling

You could move several windows and position them on the screen, but for a faster alternative, Windows XP can *tile* your windows for you automatically. Tiled windows appear side by side, either horizontally or vertically. Tiled windows can be especially handy if you need to see data in two or more windows at the same time.

To see how to tile windows, click the Start button and then click **All Programs**. Click **Accessories** and then click **Paint**. Windows XP displays the Paint window on the screen.

Click the Start button and then click **All Programs**. Click **Accessories** and then click **WordPad**. Windows XP displays the WordPad window on the screen.

Right-click any blank spot on the taskbar. A menu pops up. Click **Tile Windows Horizontally**. Windows XP displays your two program windows stacked on top of each other.

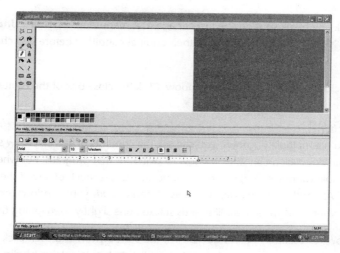

Figure 5-10 *Windows tiled horizontally appear stacked one on top of the other.*

Right-click any blank spot on the taskbar again. A menu pops up. Click **Tile Windows Vertically**. Windows XP displays your two program windows side by side.

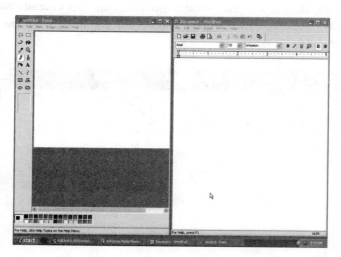

Figure 5-11 *Windows tiled vertically appear side by side.*

Right-click any blank spot on the taskbar again. A menu pops up. Click **Undo Tile**. Windows XP displays the windows in their original condition before you chose to tile them.

Click the close box of the WordPad window. Click the close box of the Paint window.

Cascading

When you tile multiple windows, you can see the contents of each window so that you can quickly click on another window to switch to that program. But when you have multiple windows tiled, you may not be able to see much of any of the windows. As another alternative, Windows XP can *cascade* your windows, which makes all your windows appear like cards stacked one slightly overlapping the other.

To see how to cascade your windows, click the Start button and then click **All Programs**. Click **Accessories** and then click **Paint**. Windows XP displays the Paint window on the screen.

Click the Start button and then click **All Programs**. Click **Accessories** and then click **WordPad**. Windows XP displays the WordPad window on the screen.

Right-click any blank spot on the taskbar. A menu pops up. Click **Cascade Windows**. Windows XP displays your two program windows with one program window slightly covering the other.

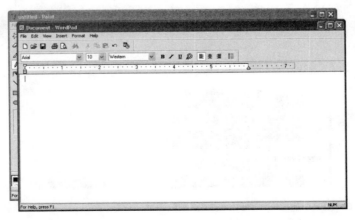

Figure 5-12 *Cascaded windows appear one slightly behind the other.*

When you cascade your windows, you can switch to another window by clicking on the title bar of that program window.

Click the close box of the WordPad window. Click the close box of the Paint window.

> **AS A MATTER OF FACT**   *After you cascade your windows, you can always move or resize them.*

Quitting a Program

When you're done with a program, it's a good idea to exit or quit that program. Not only will this free up memory and help make your computer work faster, but it also avoids cluttering up your desktop with too many windows.

Before you quit any program, you should first save any data in that program. To save data in most programs, click the **File** menu and then click **Save**, or just press **CTRL+S**.

Closing a Program Gently

Once you have saved data in a program window, you can close it. You typically can quit a program in one of four ways: click the close box of the program window, press **ALT+F4**, click the **File Exit** or **Quit**, or right-click the program button on the taskbar and choose **Close**.

Figure 5-13   *You can close any program from the taskbar.*

To see how to quit a program, click the Start button and then click **All Programs**. Click **Accessories** and then click **WordPad**. Windows XP displays the WordPad window on the screen.

Press **ALT+F4**. The WordPad window goes away. Click the Start button again and then click **All Programs**. Click **Accessories** and then click **WordPad**. Windows XP displays the WordPad window once more on the screen. Click the **File** menu and then click **Exit**.

Killing a Program

The more you use a computer, the more you'll learn that nothing ever works 100 percent correctly all the time. One common problem that you may face occurs when a program suddenly stops working for no apparent reason. The program may appear on the screen but refuses to respond to any mouse clicks or keyboard commands you give it. When a program appears frozen in a catatonic state, the program is said to have *crashed*. When a program crashes, you won't be able to close that program's window the usual way. Instead, you have to resort to the Task Manager.

To see how the Task Manager works, click the Start button again and then click **All Programs**. Click **Accessories** and then click **WordPad**. Windows XP displays the WordPad window on the screen.

Right-click a blank part of the taskbar. When a menu appears, click **Task Manager**. The Windows Task Manager appears and displays all the different programs currently loaded on your computer under the Task list.

Figure 5-14
The Task Manager shows you all the programs running on your computer.

Click the WordPad program under the task list and then click **End Task**. The Task Manager closes WordPad. Click the close box of the Task Manager to make it go away.

> **AS A MATTER OF FACT**   *If you click Switch Task, you can switch to another currently running program. If you click New Task, you can load a new program.*

Removing (Uninstalling) a Program

After you have installed several programs, you may find that you no longer need one or more programs. While you could leave programs stored on your computer indefinitely, you may want to remove a program to free up more space on your hard disk. Sometimes if you have an old version of a program and want to install a new one, you may need to uninstall or remove the old version of that program first.

AS A MATTER OF FACT   *Never delete programs from your computer using the Windows Explorer. If you delete program files, you may confuse Windows XP and cause problems with your computer.*

You can choose two different ways to remove or uninstall a program from your computer. Many programs come with their own uninstall program. If the program you want to remove comes with such a program, run that uninstall program.

AS A MATTER OF FACT   *The following steps show you how to uninstall a program from your computer. If you do not have a program you want to uninstall, do not follow the steps all the way through.*

If a program does not come with its own uninstall program, then you can use the Windows XP uninstall program feature instead. To see how to uninstall a program, click the Start button and then click **Control Panel**. The Control Panel window appears.

Click Add or Remove Programs. The Add or Remove Programs window appears and lists all the programs currently installed on your computer.

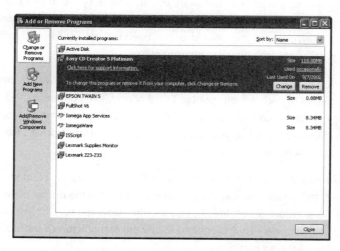

Figure 5-15   *The Add or Remove Programs window lets you remove any program installed on your computer.*

Click the program that you want to uninstall. Windows XP tells you the size of the program so that you know how much space you will regain on your hard disk if you delete this program, how often you've used this program, and the last time you used it.

Click Change/Remove. A dialog box appears and asks if you really want to delete your chosen program. Click Yes. Windows XP uninstalls your chosen program.

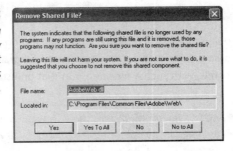

Figure 5-16
Removing a program may delete files that other programs may need.

Sometimes Windows XP may ask if you want to keep or delete a file. If you delete a file, you may prevent other programs from working. If you keep the file, you will clutter up your hard disk with useless files. Unless you're absolutely sure, click No to All to tell Windows XP not to delete any files that may be shared with other programs.

Adding Equipment

When you connect any piece of hardware to your computer, such as a printer, scanner, or joystick, Windows XP may not know how to use that equipment. So one additional type of program that you may need to install consists of *software drivers* (also called drivers) for your equipment.

A driver is a special program that tells Windows XP how to work with a specific piece of equipment such as your printer. Every printer, even different models made by the same manufacturer, needs its own driver. Most drivers come included with your equipment on a CD, but you can also download the latest drivers from the manufacturer's web site.

When you connect a new piece of equipment to your computer, Windows XP can often identify this equipment and then prompt you to install the proper driver for that equipment (see Figure 5-17). Ideally, you should follow the specific instructions that come with your new equipment and follow the manufacturer's instructions to install the driver for your computer.

Figure 5-17
Windows XP can recognize a new piece of equipment.

Sometimes you may need to install a driver manually. To see how to install a printer driver, click the Start button and then click **Control Panel**. When the Control Panel window appears, click **Printers and Other Hardware**. The Printers and Other Hardware window appears.

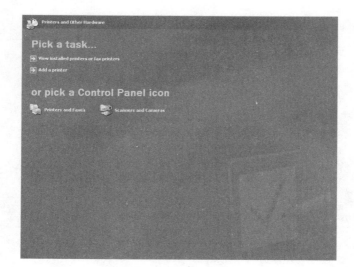

Figure 5-18   *You must install drivers for different equipment such as a printer or joystick.*

Click Add a printer. The Add Printer Wizard dialog box appears. At this point, you can just follow the instructions that this dialog box gives you to install the proper driver for your printer. Click Cancel and then click the close box of the Printers and Faxes window to make it go away.

6

Have Fun

Nobody really wants to buy a computer just to balance their checkbook or calculate their income taxes. Most people think computers are pretty dull unless they can have fun with them. So to keep you amused, Windows XP can turn your computer into a radio, a stereo, a photo album, a video game console, and even a movie theater so you can watch the latest DVD releases on your personal computer.

While you may be perfectly happy listening to music through the Internet or from your own audio CD collection, Windows XP also gives you the chance to copy your favorite songs from different CDs and store and arrange them exactly the way you want on a separate CD that you can play on your computer or on a separate CD player anywhere else.

If you have a digital camera, you'll find that Windows XP makes it easy for you to copy images from your camera to your computer so you can store, view, and edit them. If you have a digital video camera, you can even store and edit your home movies on Windows XP.

With so many different ways to use Windows XP for fun, now you have no excuse for being bored with your computer, so you just have to deal with being bored at work instead.

Playing Games

Windows XP includes several games that can keep you amused on a rainy day. While the games may not be as challenging or graphically impressive as the more advanced commercial games you can buy from a store, Windows XP's games are much easier to play the next time you need to spend a little time on a mindless diversion while you wait for your computer to finish printing or downloading a file over the Internet.

To find the Windows XP games, click the Start button, click **All Programs**, and then click **Games**. A menu appears that lists all the different games available (see Figure 6-1). Click a game, such as Solitaire or Minesweeper. Your chosen game appears in its own window.

> *AS A MATTER OF FACT*   To find out how to play a game, start the game you want to play and then press **F1**. The game displays a help file that explains how to play the game.

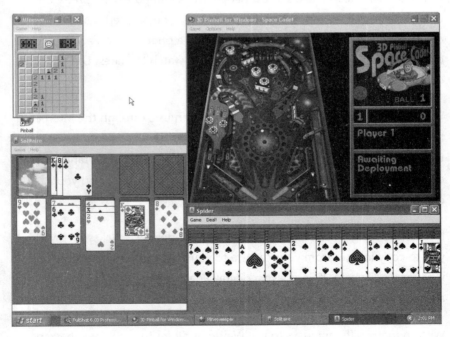

Figure 6-1   *Windows XP comes with several games you can play.*

Click the close box of the game window to make it go away.

Playing Music

As long as you have a sound card connected to a pair of speakers, you can use Windows XP to play music on your computer using a program called the Windows Media Player. The Windows Media Player can play music from two sources: compact discs (CDs) and audio files that you can copy off the Internet or share with others.

Loading a CD

When you put a CD in your computer, Windows XP automatically assumes that you want to do something with it. Most of the time, Windows XP can recognize an audio CD and start playing it right away with the Windows Media Player.

Sometimes Windows XP won't recognize an audio CD, so when this happens, Windows XP displays a dialog box that asks what you want to do with the CD. To play an audio CD, just click the Play audio CD icon and click OK.

Figure 6-2
Windows XP may display a dialog box asking you what to do with a CD it doesn't recognize.

Playing a CD

Normally when you insert an audio CD into your computer, the Windows Media Player starts playing your CD right away. In case it doesn't start playing your CD, click the Play button (see Figure 6-3).

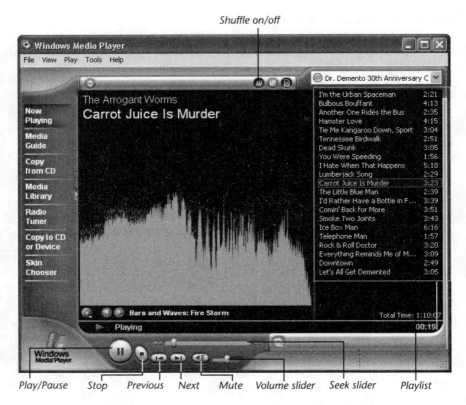

Shuffle on/off

Play/Pause   Stop   Previous   Next   Mute   Volume slider   Seek slider   Playlist

Figure 6-3   *The controls to the Windows Media Player mimic an ordinary VCR or tape recorder controls.*

To see how the Windows Media Player works, insert an audio CD in your computer. The Windows Media Player appears and starts playing the first song of your CD. If the first song does not start playing, click the Play button.

After you click the Play button, it turns into a Pause button. Click the Pause button and Windows Media Player temporarily stops playing your song. Notice that the Pause button has turned into the Play button. To start playing your music again, click the Play button once more. Click the Mute button. Notice that Windows Media Player continues playing your music but cuts off the sound. Click the Mute button again to turn off the Mute feature.

Click the Stop button. The Windows Media Player stops playing your music. Click the Next button. Windows Media highlights the next song in the playlist. Click the Previous button. The Windows Media Player highlights the immediately previous song in the playlist.

As an alternative to hearing the same songs in the same order all the time, click the Shuffle button and then click the Play button. Click the Next button and the Windows Media Player highlights a different song, out of order, in the playlist.

Click the Play button. Move the mouse pointer over the Volume slider and drag the slider left and right to adjust the volume. Release the left mouse button when you're happy with the volume level.

Move the mouse pointer over the Seek slider, drag the slider left, and release the left mouse button. When you move the slider to the left, you can hear the beginning of the song. If you move the slider to the right, you can hear the ending of the song.

Click the close box of the Windows Media Player to make it go away.

Getting Album Information

If you're connected to the Internet, the Windows Media Player can download a track listing of your CD so that you can see the names of both the album and the individual song titles. If the Windows Media Player doesn't list your album name and songs, or if the album or song names are incorrect, you can tell the Windows Media Player to download the latest information from WindowsMedia.com.

To get the latest information about your audio CD, click Copy from CD and then click Get Names (see Figure 6-4). Then click Search. The Windows Media Player displays a Search for album information dialog box.

Click the Search by artist name or Search by album name radio button. Type an album or artist name in the text box that appears and then click Next. You may need to click on one or more radio buttons until you find the correct album name for your audio CD. When you finally find the correct album name, click Finish.

Figure 6-4 *The Windows Media Player can search the Internet for the correct album and song names for your audio CD.*

Playing an Audio File

Besides playing music stored on audio CDs, the Windows Media Player can also play audio files, such as audio files of music that you can download off the Internet or files you copied off an audio CD.

Playing a Single File

To see how to play an audio file, click the Start button, click **All Programs**, and then click **Windows Media Player**. The Windows Media Player window appears.

Click the **File** menu and then click **Open**. An Open dialog box appears. Click the Look in list box and click My Documents. Double-click the My Music folder. Then double-click the Sample Music folder.

> **AS A MATTER OF FACT** *Windows XP provides a special My Music folder for storing audio files. Although you can store audio files anywhere you want, if you store audio files in the My Music folder, you'll always know where to find them again.*

Click an audio file and then click Open. Click the Play button to hear your audio file. Click the Stop button when you're done, or just wait until the audio file is done playing. Click the close box of the Windows Media Player.

Creating a Playlist

When you load and play a single audio file, the Windows Media Player plays that file and then stops. If you want to play several audio files one after another, you need to create a playlist, which simply tells the Windows Media Player, "See this list of audio files? I want you to play all of them." By using playlists, you can arrange your favorite songs in a group and listen to them whenever you want.

To see how to create a playlist, click the Start button, click **All Programs**, and then click **Windows Media Player**. The Windows Media Player window appears. Click Media Library. The Windows Media Player displays a media library list in the left pane and a title listing in the right pane.

New playlist button   Media library pane   Title listing pane

Figure 6-5 You can create and play your own playlists of songs.

Click the New playlist button. A New Playlist dialog box appears. Click in the text box, type a name for your playlist, and then click OK. Your newly created playlist name appears in the Media library pane under the My Playlists category.

Adding Items to a Playlist

Once you've created a playlist, you'll need to add audio files to that list. To do this, click the Start button, click **All Programs**, and then click **Windows Media Player**. The Windows Media Player window appears. If a plus sign appears to the left of the Audio category in the Media library pane, click the plus sign to display the Audio category.

Click the Audio category. The track listing pane displays all the audio files stored in your My Music folder. Right-click an audio file. A pop-up menu appears. Click **Add to Playlist**. An Add to Playlist dialog box appears. Click the name of your playlist and click OK. Repeat these steps for each audio file that you want to add to the playlist.

> **AS A MATTER OF FACT** *For a faster method, you can click the name of an audio file and drag that filename to your playlist.*

Listening to a Playlist

To listen to a playlist, click the Start button, click **All Programs**, and then click **Windows Media Player**. The Windows Media Player window appears. Click Media Library. If a plus sign appears to the left of the My Playlists category in the Media library pane, click the plus sign to display the My Playlists category.

Click a playlist name. The track listing pane displays all the audio files that make up that playlist. Click the Play button.

> **AS A MATTER OF FACT** *When you listen to a playlist, you can also click the Shuffle on button to play the audio files in your playlist in randomly chosen order.*

Removing Items from a Playlist

Sometimes you may want to remove an item from the playlist. To do this, click the Start button, click **All Programs**, and then click **Windows Media Player**. The Windows Media Player window appears. If a plus sign appears to the left of the My Playlists category in the Media library pane, click the plus sign to display the My Playlists category.

Click the name of the playlist that contains the audio file you want to remove. The track listing pane displays all the audio files stored in your My Music folder. Right-click an audio file. A pop-up menu appears. Click **Delete from Playlist**. Repeat these steps for each audio file that you want to delete from the playlist.

AS A MATTER OF FACT *When you delete a file from a playlist, you aren't actually deleting the file; you're just deleting its name from the playlist.*

Copying from a CD

Sometimes you may have an audio CD with just one or two great songs on it. Rather than listen to a bunch of mediocre songs just to get to the good ones, just copy the good songs off your audio CD and store them in your My Music folder. Once you've stored your favorite songs in your My Music folder, you can create a playlist (see the preceding section) so that you can listen to all the best songs from your CDs.

To see how you can copy songs from a CD to your My Music folder, put an audio CD into your computer. Windows XP immediately loads the Windows Media Player and plays the first song.

Copy Music button

Figure 6-6 *The Windows Media Player can copy your favorite songs from a CD.*

Click Copy from CD. The Windows Media Player shows a list of all the tracks available on your CD. If a check mark appears to the left of a song, that means that the Windows Media Player will copy that song to your My Music folder. If you do not want to copy a particular song, click in the check box to clear the check mark (see Figure 6-7).

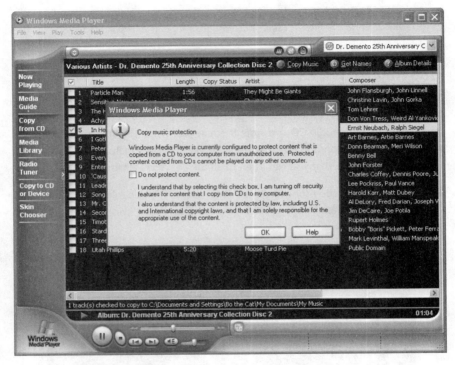

Figure 6-7 *The Windows Media Player can prevent copied songs from playing on other computers.*

Click Copy Music. The Windows Media Player displays a dialog box that warns about copyright restrictions. If a check mark appears in the Do not protect content check box, you will be able to copy and play your songs on any other computer.

Click OK. The Windows Media Player copies your selected songs to your My Music folder.

Listening to Radio

When you get tired of listening to your same audio CDs, you can listen to audio files that you can download off the Internet. But for greater variety, you can use the Windows Media Player to listen to some of your favorite radio stations on your computer instead.

> **AS A MATTER OF FACT** *To listen to radio stations, you need to connect to the Internet.*

Tuning in to a Station

The Windows Media Player gets its list of available radio stations from the WindowsMedia.com web site, so the list of radio stations may change. To listen to a radio station, click the Start button, click **All Programs**, and then click **Windows Media Player**. The Windows Media Player window appears.

Click Radio Tuner. The Windows Media Player shows three panes. One pane organizes radio stations into lists. The second pane lists radio stations by category, such as Rock or Jazz. The third pane lists the current hits.

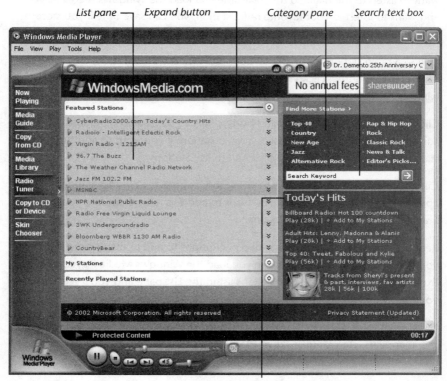

List pane — Expand button — Category pane — Search text box

Today's Hits pane

Figure 6-8 *The Windows Media Player gives you several ways to choose a radio station.*

Click the Expand button in the Featured Stations list in the List pane. A list of radio stations appears. Click Top 40 in the Category pane. The Windows Media Player displays a list of radio stations in the Top 40 category. Click Return to My Stations.

Click a radio station listed under the Today's hits pane. The Windows Media Player plays your chosen radio station.

> **AS A MATTER OF FACT** *You may have to wait a minute or two before you hear anything while the Windows Media Player downloads the audio of your chosen radio station from the Internet.*

Click the close box of the Windows Media Player when you're done.

Saving a Station

With so many radio stations to choose from, chances are good that you won't want to listen to them all. So the next time you load the Windows Media Player and want to listen to your favorite radio station, you can save time if you store your favorite radio stations in the My Stations list.

To add a radio station to the My Stations list, click the Start button, click **All Programs**, and then click **Windows Media Player**. The Windows Media Player window appears.

Click Radio Tuner. Click the Expand button next to the Featured Stations list. When a list of radio stations appears, click a radio station. If you want to add this radio station to your My Stations list, click Add to My Stations.

Click a category, such as Jazz, in the Category pane. A list of radio stations appears. Click a radio station. If you want to add this radio station to your My Stations list, click Add to My Stations.

Repeat the steps in the preceding two paragraphs to add as many radio stations to your My Stations list. The next time you load the Windows Media Player, click the Expand button next to the My Stations list in the List pane and you'll see a list of your favorite radio stations stored there.

If you want to delete a song from your playlist, right-click that song and when a menu appears, click **Delete from Playlist**.

> **AS A MATTER OF FACT** *When you delete a song from a playlist, you won't delete the actual audio file; you just remove the song's name from the playlist.*

Click the close box of the Windows Media Player when you're done.

Customization

Just for fun, you can customize the way the Windows Media Player looks and sounds. The simplest way to change the appearance of the Windows Media Player is to hide the menu bar.

Show/Hide menu bar button

Figure 6-9 *The Windows Media Player with and without its menu bar.*

To hide the menu bar, click the Show/Hide menu bar button. The Windows Media Player hides the menu bar from view. To display the menu bar again, click the Show/Hide menu bar button once more.

Visualizations

A visualization is nothing more than a geometric pattern of colors that changes as your music plays. Visualizations serve no practical purpose; they're just fun to look at. To choose a visualization, click the Start button, click **All Programs**, and then click **Windows Media Player**. The Windows Media Player window appears (see Figure 6-10).

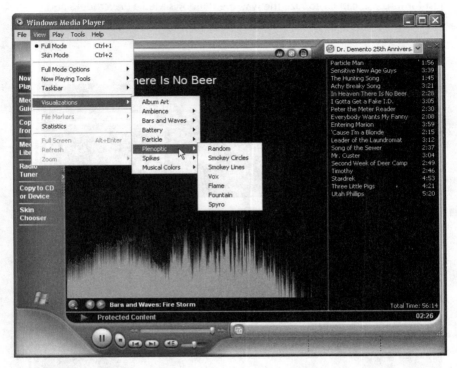

Figure 6-10 *The Windows Media Player provides lots of images to keep you amused while listening to music.*

Click the **View** menu and then click **Visualizations**. A menu appears that lists different categories such as Ambience or Particle. Click one of these categories and another menu appears that lists all the visualizations for that particular category. Click the visualization you want. Insert an audio CD in your computer and watch as the visualization changes while each song plays.

> ***AS A MATTER OF FACT*** *If you click the **Tools** menu and then choose* ***Download visualizations***, *you can download more visualizations from the WindowsMedia.com web site.*

Skins

A *skin* completely changes the way the Windows Media Player looks. These skins range from the unique to the totally bizarre, so you can choose the skin that best suits your mood at the moment.

> **AS A MATTER OF FACT** *When you change the Windows Media Player skin, the controls, such as the Play and Stop buttons, may appear in wildly different positions. Just move the mouse pointer over a button and a little help window pops up to tell you what that button does.*

To choose a skin for the Windows Media Player, click the Start button, click **All Programs**, and then click **Windows Media Player**. The Windows Media Player window appears.

Apply Skin button   More Skins button

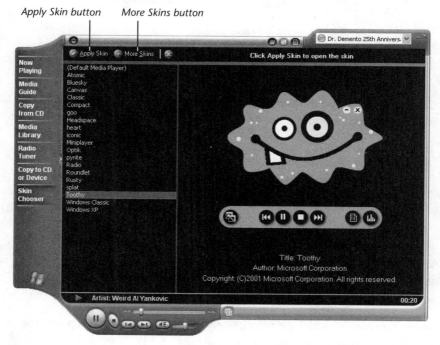

Figure 6-11 *You can change the Windows Media Player look by choosing a different skin.*

Click Skin Chooser. The Windows Media Player shows you a preview of your chosen skin. Click Apply Skin.

To change the Windows Media Player skin, click the **View** menu and then click **Skin Mode**, or press **CTRL+2**. The Windows Media Player changes into your chosen skin and displays a window to the bottom right-hand corner of your screen, as shown in this figure.

Figure 6-12
The Windows Media Player can appear with a bizarre skin.

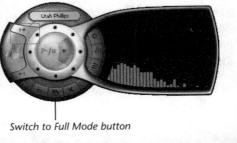

Switch to Full Mode button

Click the Switch to full mode button or press **CTRL+1**. The Windows Media Player returns to its normal appearance.

Adjusting the Sound Quality

While listening to your music, you may want to make some minor adjustments in the sound. Your speakers might allow you to do this, but you can also adjust the sound through the Windows Media Player.

To see how you can adjust the sound, insert an audio CD in your computer. The Windows Media Player window appears (see Figure 6-13).

Show/Hide Equalizer and Settings button

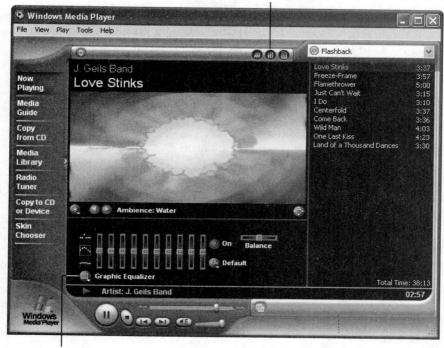

Select View button

Figure 6-13 You can use the equalizer in the Windows Media Player to adjust the sound quality.

Click the Show equalizer and settings button. Click the Select view button and when a menu appears, click **Graphic Equalizer**. A series of vertical sliders appears. Drag the sliders up or down to adjust the sound quality. When you're done, click the Show/Hide equalizer and settings button again to hide the graphic equalizer from view.

Storing Digital Photos

With so many people buying scanners and digital cameras, Windows XP now includes features to save and display your digital images. That way, when you need to find a certain image again, you don't have to remember the exact name you gave the file; you can just browse through miniature versions of your digital images so that you can find the one you want.

Getting Pictures into Your Computer

To store a picture on your computer, you need a scanner, a digital camera, or an Internet connection. Scanners are great when you want to capture images from printed material such as old photographs, books, magazines, or newspapers. Digital cameras can capture any type of image that you see, such as landscapes or family portraits. Even if you don't have a scanner or a digital camera, you can still capture images off the Internet and store them on your computer.

Scanning an Image

Even though your scanner may have come with its own software, Windows XP can often recognize and work with many different scanner models. To see how to scan in a picture, make sure you have connected your scanner to your computer, click the Start button, and then click **Control Panel**. The Control Panel window appears.

Click Printers and Other Hardware and then click Scanners and Cameras. The Scanners and Cameras window appears.

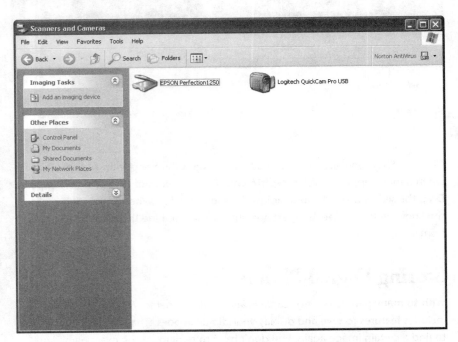

Figure 6-14 *The Scanners and Cameras window lists all the scanners and cameras connected to your computer.*

Place an item on your scanner and then double-click the scanner icon in the Scanners and Cameras window. A Scanner and Camera Wizard dialog box appears. Click Next. The Scanner and Camera Wizard dialog box displays several radio buttons that give you a choice on how you want to scan in your image, such as in color or black and white.

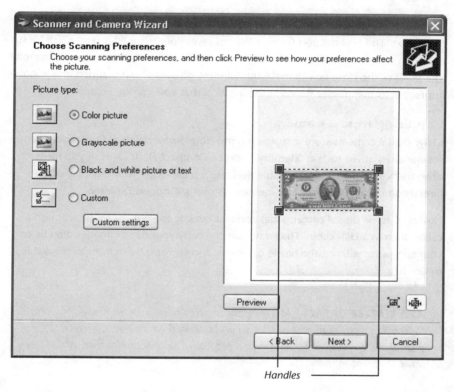

Handles

Figure 6-15 *The Scanner and Camera Wizard lets you preview your image before you save it.*

Click a radio button and then click Preview. If you just want to capture part of the scanned image, move the mouse pointer over one of the corner handles and drag the mouse to increase or decrease the part of the image that you want to save.

Click Next. The Scanner and Camera Wizard dialog box asks you for a filename and a destination to store your scanned image. Type a descriptive name for the file and click the folder and the drive where you want to store your image.

Click Next. The Scanner and Camera Wizard saves your scanned image. Click Next and then click Finish. Windows XP displays a window that shows you your scanned image. Click the close box to make this window go away. Your scanned image now appears in its own folder stored in the location that you specified earlier.

Capturing from a Camera

Many digital cameras store images on removable devices such as floppy disks or smaller alternatives such as Memory Sticks or Compact Flash cards. If you have a drive that can read these removable devices, you can copy your digital images directly off these removable storage devices using Windows Explorer.

However, some digital cameras can connect directly to your computer through a cable, such as a USB cable. That way, you can copy your digital images directly to your computer without the hassle of storing and copying them from a removable device first.

To see how you can retrieve images from a digital camera, connect a digital camera to your computer, click the Start button, click **Control Panel**, click **Printers and Other Hardware**, and then click **Scanners and Cameras**. The Scanners and Cameras window appears.

Double-click the icon that represents your digital camera. A Scanner and Camera Wizard dialog box appears. Click Next. The Scanner and Camera Wizard dialog box displays miniature pictures of your digital images (see Figure 6-16).

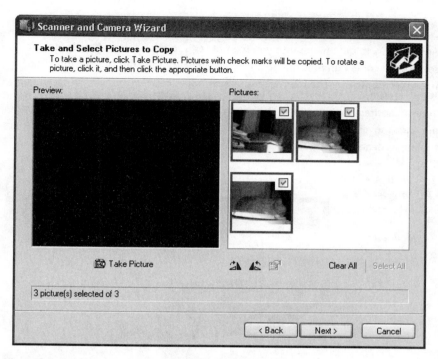

Figure 6-16 *You can browse and select the digital images you want to copy from your camera to your computer.*

Click on the digital image you want to copy. You can select two or more pictures if you hold down the **CTRL** key and then click on a digital image. Click Next. The Scanner and Camera Wizard dialog box asks for a name for your digital images and a location where you want to store them.

Type a name for your group of pictures and then click Browse. A Browse dialog box appears. Click the drive and the folder where you want to store your digital images and then click OK. Click Next.

Windows XP copies your chosen images. The Scanner and Camera Wizard dialog box asks what you want to do now. Make sure the Nothing, I'm finished working with these pictures radio button is chosen and click Next.

The Scanner and Camera Wizard dialog box tells you how many files it copied. Click Finish.

Saving from the Web

Another way to get images into your computer is to copy them off web sites. To see how to copy a graphic image off a web site, click the Start button and click **Internet Explorer**. The Internet Explorer window appears.

Type an address such as **www.theonion.com** and press **ENTER**. When a web page appears, move the mouse pointer over a graphic image. After a few moments, a toolbar appears.

Figure 6-17
The Image toolbar lets you copy and save graphic images off a web page.

Save   Print   E-mail   Open My Pictures folder

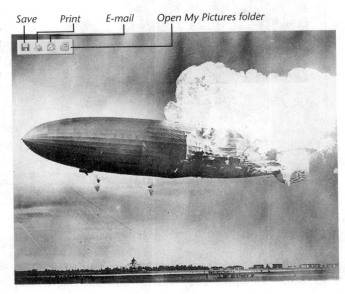

AS A MATTER OF FACT   *For a faster way to copy images off web pages, right-click on the image and when a menu appears, click **Save Picture As**.*

Click Save. A Save Picture dialog box appears. Click in the file name text box and type a name for the image and then click Save. Windows XP saves your graphic image in your chosen folder. Click the close box of the Internet Explorer window.

AS A MATTER OF FACT   *Be careful about using images that you copy off web sites, since those images may be copyrighted.*

Viewing Your Pictures

Once you've stored digital images on your computer, you can use Windows Explorer (see Chapter 3) to browse through your images. Windows Explorer provides two ways to view your digital images: Filmstrip and Thumbnail views.

The Filmstrip view displays your digital images in a horizontal strip and lets you enlarge one image at a time. You can also rotate images in case they don't appear oriented correctly.

The Thumbnail view displays miniature pictures of your images so that you can find the image you want at a glance. When you have a lot of images to browse through, the Thumbnail view is best, since it can display more images on the screen at the same time.

To see what the Filmstrip and Thumbnail views look like, click the Start button and click **All Programs**. When a menu appears, click **Accessories** and then click **Windows Explorer**. The Windows Explorer window appears.

Click the My Pictures folder, which is stored inside the My Documents folder. Windows Explorer displays the contents of the My Pictures folder. Click the **View** menu and click **Filmstrip**. Windows Explorer displays the Filmstrip view and shows the enlarged view of your first image.

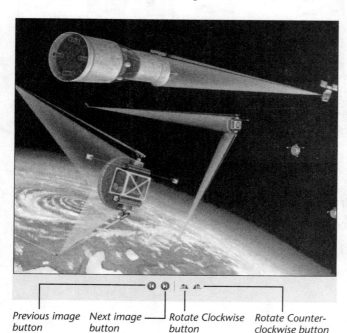

Figure 6-18
The Filmstrip view lets you see an enlarged view of a single digital image.

Previous image   Next image ──┐ Rotate Clockwise   Rotate Counter-
button   button   button   clockwise button

Click the Next image button. Windows Explorer shows you the enlarged view of the next image. Click the Rotate Clockwise button. Windows Explorer rotates your image clockwise. Click the Rotate Counterclockwise button. Windows Explorer rotates your image counterclockwise.

Click the **View** menu and click **Thumbnail**. Windows Explorer shows more of your images as smaller pictures, as shown in this figure. If you have many images stored in your My Pictures folder, you may need to click in the vertical scroll bar to browse through all your images.

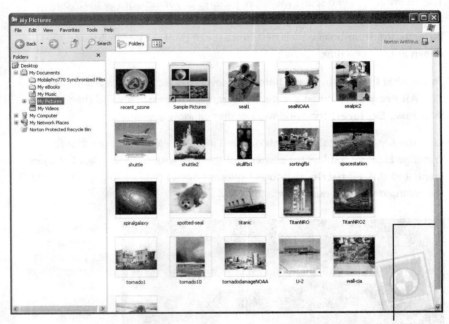

Vertical scroll bar

Figure 6-19 The Thumbnail view shows you small versions of each digital image.

AS A MATTER OF FACT The Filmstrip and Thumbnail views are the only views that let you see the contents of each digital image. If you use a different view, such as Tiles or Icons, then Windows Explorer shows your digital images as generic file icons that don't show you the contents of each file.

Viewing as a Slideshow

Once you've stored several digital images on your computer, you can show off your images through a slideshow that you can present on your computer. To view your images as a slideshow, click the Start button and click **All Programs**. When a menu appears, click **Accessories** and then click **Windows Explorer**. The Windows Explorer window appears.

Double-click the folder that contains your images, such as the My Pictures folder. If you do not see the Picture Tasks list in the left pane of the Windows Explorer window, click the Folders button. The Picture Tasks pane appears.

Folders button

Figure 6-20 *The Picture Tasks list gives you the option to view your images in a folder as a slideshow.*

Click View as slideshow under the Picture Tasks. Windows XP displays your images on the full screen (see Figure 6-21). If you move the mouse, Windows XP displays a toolbar in the upper-right corner of the screen.

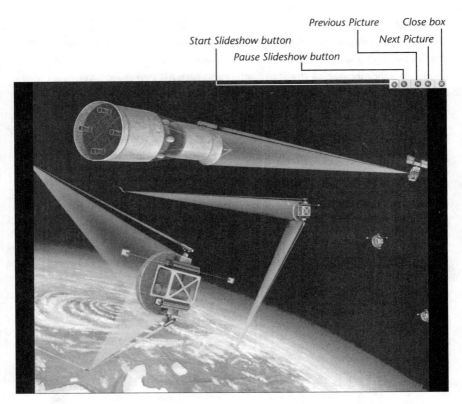

Previous Picture *Close box*
Start Slideshow button *Next Picture*
Pause Slideshow button

Figure 6-21 *The slideshow displays your images, one at a time, on the entire screen.*

Click the mouse or the Next Picture button to see the next image. Click the close box or press **ESC** to end the slide show. The Windows Explorer window appears. Click the close box.

Viewing as a Screensaver

If you like to see your images in a slideshow, you might want to turn your slideshow images into your screensaver. That way, if you don't use your computer after a certain amount of time, the screensaver starts up and displays your images one at a time on your screen.

AS A MATTER OF FACT *The Windows XP screensaver can display only digital images stored in your My Pictures folder. If you have stored your digital images in another folder, you must copy them to the My Pictures folder first before you can use those images in your screensaver.*

To see how to turn your digital images into a screensaver, click the Start button and click **Control Panel**. The Control Panel window appears. Click Appearance and Themes. The Appearance and Themes window appears.

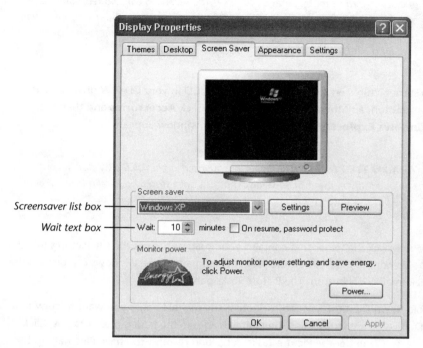

Figure 6-22 You can turn your digital images into a screensaver.

Click Choose a Screensaver. A Display Properties dialog box appears. Click in the Screensaver list box and click My Pictures Slideshow. Click the up or down arrows in the Wait text box to increase or decrease the number of minutes Windows XP waits before it turns your screensaver on. Click OK.

Click the close box of the Appearance and Themes window to make it go away. If you wait the number of minutes you specified in the Wait text box, Windows XP displays your images as a screensaver.

Storing Pictures on CD

If you have a rewritable CD drive, often abbreviated as CD+RW, you can copy and save your digital images on a CD. Since digital images can gobble up large chunks of hard disk space, you may want to store your digital images on a CD to clear off hard disk space or just to make sure you always have a backup of your digital images in case anything happens to your hard disk.

To store pictures on a CD, insert a rewritable CD in your CD+RW drive, click the Start button, and then click **All Programs**. Click **Accessories** and then click **Windows Explorer**. The Windows Explorer window appears.

Double-click the folder that contains your images, such as the My Pictures folder. If you do not see the Picture Tasks list in the left pane of the Windows Explorer window, click the Folders button. The Picture Tasks pane appears.

Hold down the **CTRL** key and click on all the digital images you want to copy to a CD. If you want to select all the digital images in the folder, press **CTRL+A**. Click Copy to CD under the Picture Tasks. A balloon reading You have files waiting to be written to the CD pops up in the lower-right corner of the screen.

Click the balloon. A CD drive window appears that shows you the files you have chosen to copy to a CD. Click Write these files to CD. A CD Wizard dialog box appears that asks for the name of your CD.

Type a name and click Next. Windows XP copies your chosen files to the CD and displays another CD Wizard dialog box when it's done. Click Finish.

Making a Movie

If you have a digital video camera, you may be able to connect it to your computer and edit your video with the Windows Movie Maker. Basically, there are three steps to using the Windows Movie Maker. First, you have to load the video into Windows Movie Maker. When you load a video, Windows Movie Maker divides your video into separate parts called clips, where each clip represents a change of scenes.

Second, you arrange your clips in sequential order, known as a timeline. Third, you can trim each clip to cut out the parts you don't want to use. When you're done, you can save your edited video to show your friends.

Loading a Video

To see how to edit a movie, click the Start button and then click **All Programs**. When a menu appears, click **Accessories** and then click **Windows Movie Maker**. The Windows Movie Maker window appears.

Click the **File** menu and then click **Import**. An Import dialog box appears. Double-click the My Videos folder, which is located inside the My Documents folder. Click Windows Movie Maker Sample File and click Open. Windows Movie Maker loads the video file and divides it into clips.

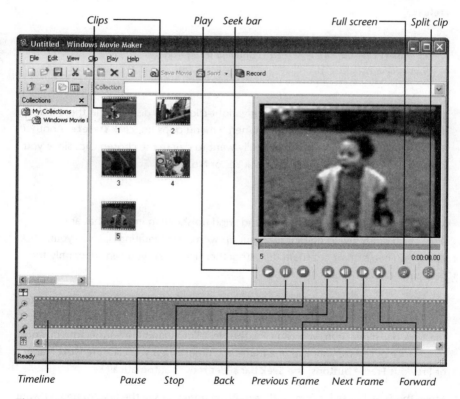

Figure 6-23 *You can arrange the parts of your video to highlight the best features of your images.*

Arranging Your Clips

Once you've loaded a video into the Windows Movie Maker, you can arrange them on the timeline. The timeline shows you which clips play first, second, third, etc.

To see how the timeline works, move the mouse pointer over the clip numbered 1 and drag it to the first spot on the timeline. Then drag the clip numbered 3 over the second spot on the timeline. Finally, drag the clip numbered 5 to the third position on the timeline.

To see how you can move a clip to a new location, drag the last clip and move the mouse pointer in between the first and second clips. When a black vertical line appears between the two clips, release the mouse button.

To see how to delete a clip, right-click the last clip. When a menu pops up, click **Delete**.

> **AS A MATTER OF FACT** *When you delete a clip from the timeline, you don't physically erase the clip.*

If you want to delete a clip permanently, right-click a clip displayed in the middle of the Windows Movie Maker window. When a menu pops up, click **Delete**. Another dialog box pops up and asks if you really want to delete the chosen clip, since you won't be able to undo this action. Click Yes or No.

Trimming Your Clips

Many times, a clip may be too long and wind up showing images that are distracting or annoying. Rather than put up with these irritating flaws in your video, you can trim or cut them out altogether. That way, you can show only the best parts of each clip.

To see how to trim a clip, click the first clip on the timeline. There are two ways to tell the Windows Movie Maker where you want to trim a clip. One, you can drag the Seek bar slider. Two, you can click the Next Frame and Previous Frame buttons to advance or reverse your clip one frame at a time. When you click the Next Frame or Previous Frame buttons, the Seek bar slider moves automatically.

Move the Seek bar slider using either method until you see the first frame you want for your clip. Click the **Clip** menu and click **Set Start Trim Point**. Windows Movie Maker trims off the unwanted part of your clip.

Move the Seek bar slider using either method until you see the last frame you want for your clip. Click the **Clip** menu and click **Set End Trim Point**. Windows Movie Maker trims off the unwanted part of your clip.

> **AS A MATTER OF FACT** *If you change your mind about the trim points you set, click the* **Clip** *menu and then click* **Clear Trim Points***.*

Playing Your Clips

After you're done trimming your clips and arranging them in the order you want, you can view your work to see how it looks as a single video. Click the **Play** menu and then click **Play Entire Storyboard/Timeline**. The Windows Movie Maker plays your entire edited clips as a single video.

Saving Your Clips

When you're happy with the way your edited video looks, it's time to save it. Click the **File** menu and click **Save Movie**. A Save Movie dialog box appears, as shown here. Click in the Setting list box and choose the quality setting you want for your video, such as High Quality or Medium Quality. The higher the quality of your video, the larger the file size will be.

Setting list box

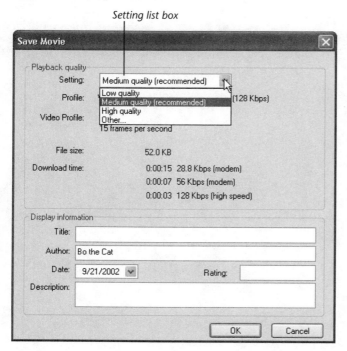

Figure 6-24
You can choose the visual quality of your video at the expense of increasing the file size.

Click OK. A Save As dialog box appears. Click in the File name text box and type a name for your video. You may also want to click in the Save in list box to choose a drive and a folder to store your video. Then click Save.

> **AS A MATTER OF FACT**   *If you click the **File** menu, click **Send Movie To**, and then click **E-mail**, Windows Movie Maker saves your video file and then loads your e-mail program and automatically attaches your video file to a new e-mail message. All you have to do is type in an e-mail address and any message you want to include.*

7

Enhance Windows XP

Like most types of machines, computers need regular maintenance to keep them working correctly. Sometimes this maintenance can be relatively minor, such as deleting unused files, and sometimes the maintenance can be major, such as restoring your computer after it crashes and no longer starts up correctly.

By maintaining your computer on a regular basis, you can ensure that it works when you need it. Some of the many ways that Windows XP can keep your computer tuned-up involves automatically deleting files you don't need anymore, reorganizing your hard disk so that it runs faster, automatically notifying you of the latest Windows XP updates that can keep your computer working, and even saving the data from your entire hard disk so you can recover it in case a virus or accident wipes out most of your hard disk.

For even more convenience, you can even create a schedule to tell Windows XP when to run certain maintenance tasks. By using the built-in tools that come with Windows XP, you can keep your computer running efficiently for as long as you use your computer.

Remember, maintenance on your computer is not optional. If you fail to maintain your computer, it will eventually slow down and crash on you.

Tuning Up

The more you use your computer, the more you'll crowd your hard disk with multiple files and programs. Unfortunately, the more data you store, the slower your computer works, since it needs to spend more time looking for specific data buried among other data stored on your hard disk. To speed up your computer, you can delete old files and you can reorganize the files that you want to keep.

Cleaning Up Your Disk

The simplest way to speed up your computer is to get rid of any files you no longer need. Many times when you uninstall a program, that program leaves behind several files. Sometimes when you use a program, such as a word processor, that program creates and stores temporary copies of your data on your hard disk to keep track of any changes you might have made.

All of these excess files don't hurt your computer, but they do take up space, so they can slow down your computer and keep you from storing more valuable data on your hard disk instead. While you could try to delete these files yourself, chances are good you won't know where to find them or whether these files are important or not.

So rather than guess, let Windows XP do all the hard work for you with the help of the Disk Cleanup program. The Disk Cleanup program scans your hard disk and looks for files you probably won't need, then gives you the option of deleting them.

To clean up your disk from old and unnecessary files, click the Start button, click **Control Panel**, click Performance and Maintenance, and then click Free up space on your hard disk.

> **AS A MATTER OF FACT** *You can also click the Start button, click **All Programs**, click **Accessories**, click **System Tools**, and then click **Disk Cleanup**.*

A Cleanup dialog box appears to inform you that Windows XP is scanning your hard disk for unnecessary files. When the Disk Cleanup program is done scanning your hard disk, it displays a Disk Cleanup dialog box so that you can see how much space certain files take up (see Figure 7-1). At this point, you can click in the appropriate check box to choose which files you want the Disk Cleanup program to delete.

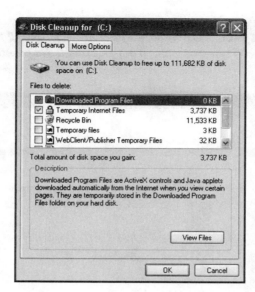

Figure 7-1
The Disk Cleanup dialog box tells you how much space different files currently waste on your hard disk.

Click in one or more check boxes to select different file types to delete, such as Temporary files or Recycle Bin. Click OK. A dialog box appears that asks if you are sure you want to delete your chosen files. Click Yes.

The Disk Cleanup dialog box appears to let you know it's busy deleting your chosen files. When the Disk Cleanup dialog box disappears, the Disk Cleanup program is done.

Reorganizing Your Disk

Every time you save data or install a program on your hard disk, your computer tries to store this information across in the same physical area of the hard disk. However, the longer you use your computer, the more you'll add and delete files, until your hard disk stores bits and pieces of different programs and data all over the place. When a hard disk can no longer store data or programs in the same physical location on the hard disk, that hard disk is said to be *fragmented*.

A fragmented hard disk slows your computer down, since your computer may need to jump around the hard disk to find all the data it needs. To keep your hard disk running smoothly, you should optimize the hard disk, which means that Windows XP yanks all the data off your hard disk and then neatly arranges them back on the hard disk again.

To see how to defragment a hard disk, click the Start button, click **Control Panel**, click **Performance and Maintenance**, and then click **Rearrange items on your hard disk** to make programs run faster. The Disk Defragmenter dialog box appears (see Figure 7-2). Click Analyze.

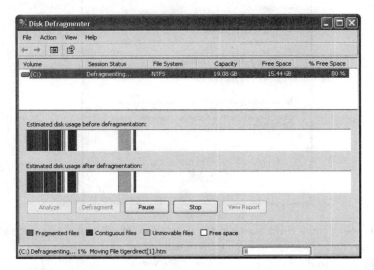

Figure 7-2 *The Disk Defragmenter program uses colors to show you how fragmented your hard disk may be.*

If your hard disk does not need defragmenting, a dialog box will appear to inform you. Click Close to make this dialog box go away. At this point, you can click the close box of the Disk Defragmenter window to make it go away.

In case your hard disk needs defragmenting or you want to defragment it anyway despite the dialog box that told you it wasn't necessary, click Defragment. Defragmenting your hard disk may take several minutes or even an hour or more, depending on the speed of your computer, the size of your hard disk, and how badly your hard disk was fragmented. Click the close box of the Disk Defragmenter window when you're done.

Restoring the Past

Despite assurances from Microsoft, Windows XP will never be 100 percent safe, although it may be more reliable than previous versions of Windows. Sometimes you may install a program that suddenly stops your computer from working. Other times, you may get a computer virus that wipes out your data. You might also edit a file and suddenly realize you wiped out some important data by mistake.

In the old days if any of this happened to you, your only option would be to cry and resolve to always make backups of your most important data in the future. But if this happens to you with Windows XP, you may still be able to recover your lost data by using the System Restore feature.

You can think of the System Restore feature as a time machine. Just use the System Restore feature and you can tell Windows XP, "Go back to three days ago, when my computer was working fine." The System Restore then restores your hard disk to exactly the same condition it had three days ago.

To use the System Restore Feature, you need to create a restore point, which is a point that you might want to return to in case your computer crashes in the future. Windows XP automatically creates restore points, but it's a good idea to make one right before you install a program or add new equipment to your computer.

Creating a Restore Point

To create a restore point, click the Start button, click **All Programs**, click **Accessories**, click **System Tools**, and then click **System Restore**. The System Restore dialog box appears.

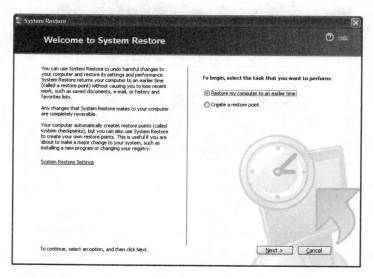

Figure 7-3 *The System Restore dialog box can let you create a restore point or return to an existing one.*

Click the Create a restore point radio button and then click Next. The System Restore dialog box asks for a descriptive name for your restore point. The name you type is for your own use only and has no effect on the creation of the restore point. Type a name and then click Create.

The System Restore dialog box tells you that you have successfully created a restore point. Click Close.

Returning to a Restore Point

If your computer starts acting erratic or simply crashes or freezes altogether, you may need to restore your computer back to a previous restore point when everything on your computer worked. First, copy all your important files to a removable disk such as a CD. Then click the Start button, click **All Programs**, click **Accessories**, click **System Tools**, and then click **System Restore**. The System Restore dialog box appears.

Click the Restore my computer to an earlier time radio button and click Next. The System Restore dialog box displays a calendar. To show you the dates of the restore points you can choose, the System Restore dialog box displays certain dates in bold.

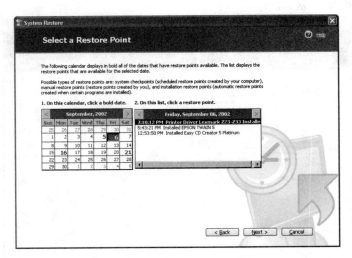

Figure 7-4   *The System Restore dialog box shows you possible restore points you can use.*

Click a restore point (a date that appears in bold) and click Next. The System Restore dialog box tells you that it will shut down and reboot. Click Next. Windows XP reboots and loads the settings defined by the restore point you chose.

The System Restore dialog box appears once more to let you know it has successfully returned your computer back to your chosen restore point. Click OK.

Scheduling

The trouble with maintaining your computer is that you need to take the time to run the disk defragmenter programs on a regular basis. Since it's likely that you'll forget or wait too long, you can just let Windows XP run these programs for you automatically.

When you tell Windows XP to run a program at a certain time on a regular basis, that's called a scheduled task. You can actually tell Windows XP to run any type of program on a regular basis, but it's especially handy to run the disk defragmenter program as a scheduled task because it can run by itself without needing any additional information from you.

Creating a Schedule

To see how to create a scheduled task, click the Start button, click **Control Panel**, click Performance and Maintenance, and then click Scheduled Tasks. The Scheduled Tasks window appears (see Figure 7-5).

> **AS A MATTER OF FACT** You can also click the Start button, click **All Programs**, click **Accessories**, click **System Tools**, and then click **Scheduled Tasks**.

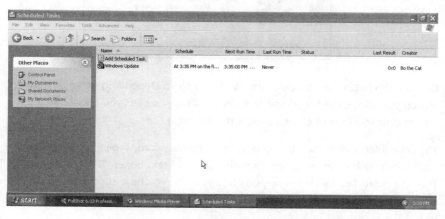

Figure 7-5 *The Scheduled Task window shows you the programs you have scheduled to run periodically.*

Double-click the Add Scheduled Task icon. A Scheduled Task Wizard dialog box appears. Click Next. The Scheduled Task Wizard dialog box lists the programs currently listed in the **All Programs** menu (see Figure 7-6).

Figure 7-6

The Scheduled Task Wizard lets you choose a program to run at a scheduled time.

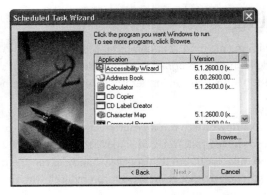

Click Windows Update and click Next. The Scheduled Task Wizard dialog box asks how often you want to run your chosen program.

Figure 7-7

You can choose to run a program daily, weekly, monthly, or when your computer starts up.

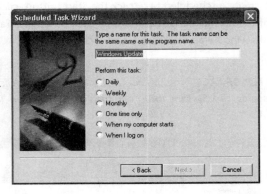

Click a radio button, such as Monthly, and click Next. Depending on which radio button you chose, the Scheduled Task Wizard dialog box lets you choose a date, day, or time to run your chosen program. Click Next.

The Scheduled Task Wizard dialog box asks for a password. Type a password in both the Enter the password and Confirm password text boxes. Then click Next. The Scheduled Task Wizard dialog box tells you that you have successfully scheduled your program to run at your chosen time. Click Finish. Click the close box of the Scheduled Task window.

Editing a Schedule Task

After you have set a schedule for one or more programs to run, you may want to edit that schedule later. To edit a scheduled task, click the Start button, click **Control Panel**, click Performance and Maintenance, and then click Scheduled Tasks. The Scheduled Tasks window appears.

Right-click the scheduled task you want to change. When a menu pops up, click **Properties**. The Properties dialog box appears.

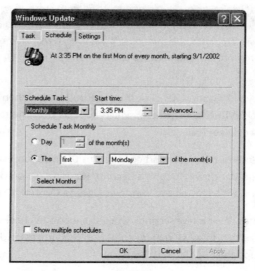

Figure 7-8
Once you've created a scheduled task, you can always modify it later.

Click the Schedule tab and make any changes to the time, day, or date that you want your scheduled task to run. Click the Settings tab and choose any other options for your scheduled task.

Click OK and then click the close box of the Scheduled Task window.

Removing a Scheduled Task

Eventually, you may want to get rid of a scheduled task altogether. To remove a program from your scheduled task list, click the Start button, click **Control Panel**, click Performance and Maintenance, and then click Scheduled Tasks. The Scheduled Tasks window appears.

Right-click the program you want to remove from your schedule. When a menu pops up, click Delete. A dialog box pops up and asks if you are sure you want to delete your scheduled task. Click Yes. Click the close box of the Scheduled Task window.

Updating

Microsoft keeps trying to make Windows XP the safest, most reliable operating system you can buy. Unfortunately, by the time you get your copy of Windows XP installed on your computer, Microsoft might have added several major changes. Fortunately, if you have an Internet connection, you can get the latest updates to Windows XP.

AS A MATTER OF FACT *Don't be too anxious to install the latest updates to Windows XP. Sometimes when you install an update, the update can actually make Windows XP less reliable, slower, and more likely to crash. Before you update Windows XP, make backup copies of all your important data and be ready to use the System Restore feature of Windows XP to return Windows XP back to the time right before you installed the update.*

To update your copy of Windows XP, click the Start button and then click **All Programs**. Click **Windows Update**, which appears near the top of the menu right above **Accessories**.

Windows XP loads Internet Explorer and connects to the Microsoft web site. The first time you run Windows Update, a Security Warning dialog box may appear to ask if you want to install the Windows Update Control. Click Yes.

Click Scan for updates. Wait a few seconds while the web site checks for the updates your copy of Windows XP may need. When this process is done, click Review and install updates.

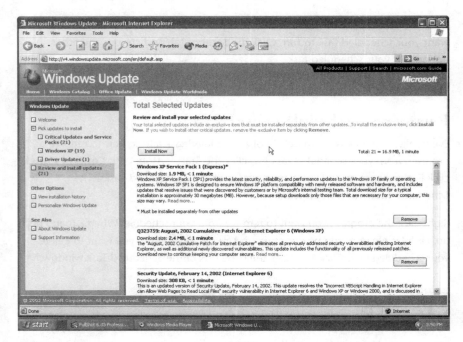

Figure 7-9 *The Microsoft web site can tell you exactly which updates your copy of Windows XP may be missing.*

There are three types of updates you may need to install: critical updates and service packs, Windows XP updates, and driver updates. Critical updates often solve problems with your computer crashing or closes security flaws that could cause hackers or viruses to crash your computer. In general, you should always install critical updates and service packs.

Windows XP updates include patches to various parts of Windows XP to make it work better or more reliably. You should install only those Windows XP updates that you absolutely need.

Driver updates include software to make your printers, video cards, sound cards, or other equipment work better and more reliably with Windows XP. In general, you should download the latest drivers for your computer.

To review and choose the different updates, click Critical Updates and Service Packs, Windows XP, or Driver Updates in the left pane of the Windows Update window. Sometimes you can install only one update separate from any other updates. This occurs most often when you must install a critical update first.

When you're done choosing the updates you want to install, click Review and install updates in the Windows Update pane. The web page lists all the updates you have chosen to install. Click Install Now.

A dialog box appears that asks if you accept the licensing terms of agreement for the updates. Click Accept. Windows XP installs your chosen updates. Sometimes you may need to reboot your computer to completely install the updates.

Increasing Accessibility

If you have limited vision or mobility, you can customize Windows XP to make your computer easier to use. To guide you through the different options available for making your computer more accessible, Windows XP provides an Accessibility Wizard.

To see how the Accessibility Wizard works, click the Start button, click **Control Panel**, and then click Accessibility Options. The Accessibility Options window appears (see Figure 7-10). Click Configure Windows to work for your vision, hearing, and mobility needs. The Accessibility Wizard dialog box appears. Click Next.

Figure 7-10

*The Accessibility
Wizard shows you
how to customize
your computer
for limited
accessibility.*

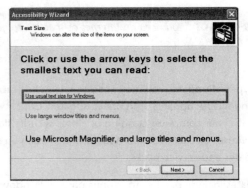

Click the text that you find most comfortable to read and then click Next. Based on what you chose, the Accessibility Wizard dialog box displays different check boxes to choose various options. Click the options you want and click Next.

The Accessibility Wizard dialog box asks you if you are blind, are deaf, or have difficulty using the keyboard or mouse. Click in the appropriate check boxes and then click Next.

Based on the options you chose, the Accessibility Wizard dialog box asks you to make other choices to determine how best to accommodate your needs. Follow the instructions in the Accessibility Wizard dialog box. When you're done making all your choices, click Finish. Depending on what choices you made, Windows XP now accommodates your needs such as by making text bigger and easier to read. Click the close box of the Accessibility Wizard window.

Magnifying

Many people find that the text on their screens may be too small to read. To make your screen easier to read, you may want to use the magnifier. To see how the magnifier works, first you need to run the Accessibility Wizard as explained in the preceding section. Then click the Start button, click **All Programs**, click **Accessories**, click **Accessibility**, and then click **Magnifier**. A dialog box appears to let you know that the magnifier can help people with poor vision but may not be adequate for people with limited vision. Click OK. The Magnifier Settings dialog box appears (see Figure 7-11).

Click in the check boxes to choose or remove any settings for the magnifier. As you move the mouse pointer, the magnifier displays an enlarged view of the area around the mouse pointer at the top of the screen.

When you're done using the magnifier, click Exit.

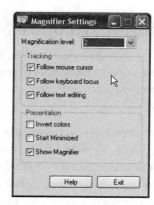

Figure 7-11
The Magnifier Settings dialog box lets you define how the magnifier works.

Typing on the Screen

If you have problems using a keyboard, you may want to use the On-Screen Keyboard, which displays a keyboard on the screen that you can type on with the mouse. To see how the On-Screen Keyboard works, click the Start button, click **All Programs**, click **Accessories**, and then click **Notepad**. The Notepad window appears.

Click the Start button, click **All Programs**, click **Accessories**, click **Accessibility**, and then click **On-Screen Keyboard**. The On-Screen Keyboard appears along with a dialog box that tells you that the On-Screen Keyboard may not be adequate for people with more restricted mobility. Click OK.

Figure 7-12 *The On-screen keyboard lets you type and press keys using the mouse.*

Click the different keys on the On-Screen Keyboard. As you click character keys, your chosen characters appear in the Notepad window. Double-click the Windows logo key. The **Start** menu appears.

Click the close box of the On-Screen Keyboard window and then click the close box of the Notepad window.

Making Multiple Accounts

If several people plan to share a single computer, you risk problems such as one person changing the desktop to some hideous color that no one else can stand, or someone accidentally erasing or moving a crucial file or program without telling anyone what they did.

To prevent these types of problems with multiple users on a single computer, you can create separate *accounts*. An account gives each person access to the computer but allows him or her to customize the computer without affecting the settings for any other user. You can even restrict what certain accounts can do. For example, you may want to restrict other accounts from accessing your important files.

There are two types of accounts: administrator and limited. An administrator account can install programs, create other accounts, and access different files on the hard disk. When you install Windows XP, the first account you create is an administrator account.

Limited accounts can only change the Windows XP appearance, such as the desktop. With a limited account, you can only use programs but may not be able to install any new ones or uninstall any existing ones.

To access each account, each user needs to define a password. If you choose a simple password, others might be able to guess that password and access your account.

Creating an Account

To see how you can create an account, click the Start button and then click **Control Panel**. When the Control Panel window appears, click **User Accounts.** The User Accounts window appears (see Figure 7-13).

Click Create a new account. A User Accounts dialog box appears and asks for a name for the account. Type in a name and click Next. The User Accounts dialog box asks you if you want to create an administrator or limited account.

Click the Computer administrator or Limited radio button and then click Create Account. The User Accounts window displays your newly created account.

Protecting an Account

Once you've created an account, you may want to password-protect it so that you'll be the only one who can use your account. Click the account that you want to protect with a password. The User Accounts window displays a list of options for your chosen account (see Figure 7-14).

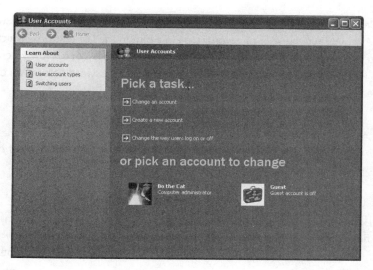

Figure 7-13 The User Accounts window lets you create or modify an account.

AS A MATTER OF FACT *If you have an administrator account, you can set and change passwords for other accounts. If you just have a limited account, you can set and change only your own password.*

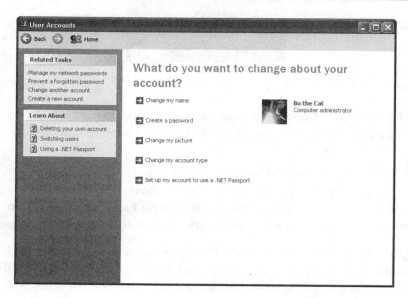

Figure 7-14 You can change the name, picture, account type, or password of any account.

Click Create a password. The User Accounts dialog box asks you to type in a password twice. After you type in your password, type in a hint in the last text box, which can remind you what your password may be. Click **Create password**. Now when you log on with your account, you must type in the correct password before you can use the computer.

> **AS A MATTER OF FACT** *If you forget your password, you will need someone with an administrator account to remove your old password and create another password for you.*

Logging on to an Account

If you have several accounts stored on your computer, you need to choose which account to use every time you start Windows XP. You can also switch accounts without rebooting.

To see how to switch accounts, click the Start button and then click **Log Off**. The Log Off Windows dialog box appears.

Figure 7-15 *The Log Off Windows dialog box lets you switch to another account.*

Click Switch User. Windows XP displays the opening screen that displays all the available accounts for your computer. Click the account name you want to use.

Modifying an Account

After you've created an account, you may need to modify it later. To modify an account, click the Start button and then click **Control Panel**. When the Control Panel window appears, click **User Accounts.** The User Accounts window appears.

Click the account you want to modify. The User Accounts window appears and lists several options for modifying that account such as Change the name or Delete the account. Click the option you want to choose. Depending on which option you choose, the User Accounts dialog box may ask you for additional information.

Power Toys

To enhance Windows XP even more, you can load special features off the Microsoft web site called Power Toys. These Power Toys are features that didn't quite make it into the official release of Windows XP, but you can add them to your computer at any time.

> **AS A MATTER OF FACT** Microsoft doesn't officially support the use of these Power Toys, even though their programmers are the ones who made them, so you can't get any technical support from Microsoft about using these Power Toys.

Some of the Power Toys available include Power Calculator, a super calculator that can graph and evaluate functions (see Figure 7-16); Tweak UI, a utility that allows you to customize Windows XP in ways not available through the normal Windows XP Control Panel; Virtual Desktop Manager, which lets you quickly switch back and forth between four different desktops; Taskbar Magnifier, which lets you access the Magnifier feature of Windows XP from the taskbar; and Webcam Timershot, which lets Windows XP take snapshots from your web cam at periodic intervals.

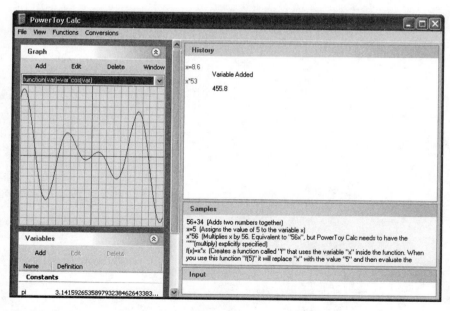

Figure 7-16 *The Power Calculator can perform relatively complicated mathematical functions.*

To install Power Toys on your computer, click the Start button and then click **Internet Explorer**. When the Internet Explorer window appears, click in the Address box, type **www.microsoft.com**, and click the Go button. The Microsoft web site appears.

Click in the Search text box, type Power Toys, and press **ENTER**. The Microsoft web site displays a link to Power Toys for Windows XP. Click this link. The Microsoft Web page lists all the Power Toys available. Click the Power Toy you want, such as the Power Calculator.

A dialog box appears and asks if you want to open or save the file. Click Open. Windows XP downloads your chosen Power Toy. An installation wizard dialog box may appear. Follow the instructions to complete the installation of your chosen Power Toy.

To learn how to run the different Power Toys, click the Start button, click **All Programs**, click **Powertoys for Windows XP**, and click **Readme**. The Readme document appears with instructions for how to use the various Power Toys.

Windows XP Shortcuts

Windows XP always gives you multiple ways to choose a command. As a novice, you may want to rely on the mouse and pull-down menus, but as you get more experienced using your computer and Windows XP, you may want a faster alternative to choose commonly used commands.

To give more experienced users a quick way to access their favorite programs, Windows XP offers a variety of shortcuts. That way, you can run your favorite programs with a single click of the mouse or a press of a key without wading through multiple layers of menus.

Besides giving you shortcuts to your programs, Windows XP also provides plenty of shortcuts to choose commonly used commands for copying data, choosing menus, and closing windows on your screen. Once you get more familiar with your computer, you'll find that all of these shortcuts to your favorite commands and programs can make Windows XP faster and easier to use than ever before.

Desktop Shortcuts

The Windows XP desktop gives you access to all the commands you need to use
your computer. Normally from the desktop, you need to click the Start button to
access different commands, but if you have a keyboard that includes the Windows
logo key, you can use that key as a shortcut instead, as shown in this table.

Press	To
CTRL+ESC	Display or hide the **Start** menu
Windows logo key	Display or hide the **Start** menu
Windows logo key+**F1**	Open the Windows Help window
Windows logo key+**E**	Open the My Computer window
Windows logo key+**BREAK**	Display the System Properties dialog box
Windows logo key+**F**	Search for a file or folder
Windows logo key+**R**	Display the Run dialog box
Windows logo key+**D**	Show the desktop

Window Management Shortcuts

Each time you start a program or open another file within the same program, your
new data appears in a separate window on your screen. If you open too many
windows, your screen can appear cluttered, so rather than allow yourself to get
buried and confused by so many windows on your screen, you can use several
shortcuts to help you keep the appearance of your windows under control.

Press	To
ALT+F4	Close the currently active window
ALT+SPACEBAR	Display the **System** menu for the active window
Windows logo key+**M**	Minimize all windows
Windows logo key+**SHIFT+M**	Restore all minimized windows
ALT+TAB	Switch to a different window

Menu Shortcuts

Every program displays all the available commands through pull-down menus.
Rather than use the mouse to click a pull-down menu, you can use the shortcuts
in Table A-1 to access menu commands instead.

Table A-1   Keyboard Shortcuts You Can Use to Access Menu Commands

Press	To
Application key	Display the shortcut menu for the selected item
SHIFT+F10	Display the shortcut menu for the selected item
F10	Highlight the first item, usually the **File** menu, on the current program's menu bar
ALT+Underlined letter in a menu title	Display the menu, such as **ALT+F** to display the **File** menu
Underlined letter in a command name on an open menu	Choose that command, such as **P** to choose the **Print** command from the **File** menu
RIGHT ARROW	Open the next menu to the right, or open a submenu
LEFT ARROW	Open the next menu to the left, or close a submenu
ESC	Cancel the current task

Dialog Box Shortcuts

Sometimes when you choose a command, such as the **Print** command, a dialog box appears. The shortcuts in this table show you how to choose an option in a dialog box using the keyboard alone without the mouse.

Table A-2   Keyboard Shortcuts You Can Use to Choose an Option in a Dialog Box

Press	To
CTRL+TAB	Move forward through tabs
CTRL+SHIFT+TAB	Move backward through tabs
TAB	Move forward through options such as buttons or check boxes
SHIFT+TAB	Move backward through options such as buttons or text boxes
ALT+Underlined letter	Choose a command or select an option
ENTER	Carry out the command for the active option or button
SPACEBAR	Select or clear the check box if the active option is a check box
Arrow keys	Select a button if the active option is a group of option buttons
F1	Display Help for the currently selected option
F4	Display the items in the currently selected list box
BACKSPACE	Open a folder one level up if a folder is selected in the Save As or Open dialog box

Editing Shortcuts

With Windows XP, you can copy or move data within a window or between two different windows, as shown in this table.

Press	To
CTRL+A	Select all items
CTRL+C	Copy the currently selected item
CTRL+X	Cut the currently selected item
CTRL+V	Paste an item previously cut or copied
CTRL+Z	Undo the previous command
DELETE	Delete the currently selected item
SHIFT+DELETE	Delete the selected item permanently without placing the item in the Recycle Bin
CTRL while dragging an item	Copy the selected item

Windows Explorer Shortcuts

When you need to manage the files on your computer, you need to use the Windows Explorer program. Like most programs, Windows Explorer offers keyboard shortcuts for choosing commonly used commands, as shown here.

Table A-3 *You Can Choose Frequently Used Commands with These Keyboard Shortcuts*

Press	To
HOME	Highlight the first item in the window
END	Highlight the last item in the window
F2	Rename the selected item
F3	Search for a file or folder
ALT+ENTER	Display the Properties window of the selected item
CTRL+SHIFT while dragging an item	Create a shortcut to the selected item
NUM LOCK+Asterisk on numeric keypad (*)	Display all subfolders under the selected folder
NUM LOCK+Plus Sign on numeric keypad (+)	Display the contents of the selected folder
NUM LOCK+Minus Sign on numeric keypad (–)	Collapse the selected folder

Table A-3 *You Can Choose Frequently Used Commands with These Keyboard Shortcuts* (continued)

Press	To
LEFT ARROW	Collapse the current selection if it's expanded, or select the parent folder
RIGHT ARROW	Display the current selection if it's collapsed, or select the first subfolder

Define a Keyboard Shortcut for Your Favorite Programs

Most likely you'll find that you use some programs practically every day. So to make starting your favorite programs faster, you can create your own shortcut keys for your programs. To avoid conflicts with any other shortcut keys, program shortcut keys must start with **CTRL+ALT** followed by an ordinary key such as a letter or number; you cannot use the **ESC**, **ENTER**, **TAB**, **SPACEBAR**, **PRINT SCREEN**, **SHIFT**, OR **BACKSPACE** keys for your program shortcut.

To define shortcuts for your favorite programs, click the Start button and click **All Programs** to display a list of all the programs currently installed on your computer. Right-click a program that you want to create a shortcut for and click **Properties**. A Properties dialog box appears.

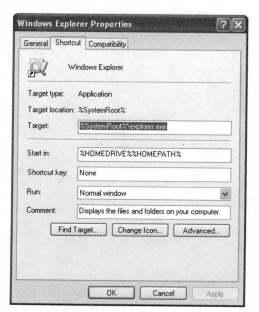

Figure A-1
The Properties dialog box lets you define a shortcut key for your favorite programs.

Click in the Shortcut text box and press a key that you want to represent your program. As soon as you type a letter or number, Windows XP automatically adds **CTRL+ALT** in front of it. So if you press **5**, your shortcut key will be **CTRL+ALT+5**.

AS A MATTER OF FACT *Every shortcut key that you create must be unique. You cannot define the same shortcut keys for two different programs.*

Click OK. Now whenever you want to run your program, you can just press the **CTRL+ALT** shortcut key combination that you defined and your chosen program immediately loads.

B

Useful Web Sites

Once you get your computer running and a few of your favorite programs installed, you may be perfectly content to do nothing more with your computer than write a few letters, play some games, or balance your checkbook. Although many people have no need or desire to do anything more, a growing number of people are finding all sorts of fascinating new uses for their computer just by connecting to the Internet. While most people use the Internet exclusively to send and receive e-mail, more and more people are discovering the wonderful world of the World Wide Web.

Through an Internet connection and the World Wide Web, you can read news from around the world; search for information about any topics that might interest you, such as UFOs, gardening, model rocketry, marathon running, or quilting; or download free programs, including games, business programs, and utilities to keep your computer running more efficiently.

Of course, you won't be able to do anything on the Internet if you don't know where to look. So to give you a hand, this appendix lists some of the more popular sites you might want to visit first that include search engines to help you find practically anything on the Internet; web sites that contain the software drivers (programs) you need to keep your printers, scanners, and graphics cards working; and web sites offering free software so you can try free and inexpensive software on your computer to save you money.

Visit a Search Engine

You can find practically anything on the Internet if you just know where to look. To find what you want on the Internet, use a search engine, which acts like a telephone directory for the Internet. Just type in a few keywords that describe what you want to find, such as "cat breeding" or "car repair," and the search engine lists dozens of web sites that contain information about your chosen topic. Now all you have to do is browse through this list of web sites until you find the information you want.

One of the most popular search engines is Yahoo! (http://www.yahoo.com). Like most search engines, Yahoo! gives you the choice to search by keywords or by browsing through different categories such as Education, Society & Culture, or Health (see Figure B-1). When you search by keyword, you may find some irrelevant web sites but also some web sites that you wouldn't necessarily find if you had searched through Yahoo!'s different categories.

Some other popular search engines include MSN.com (http://www.msn.com), AltaVista (http://www.altavista.com), Lycos (http://www.lycos.com), and Google (http://www.google.com).

Figure B-1 *Yahoo! offers e-mail and Internet access in addition to its search capabilities.*

One problem with search engines is that they may find different web sites. For example, you can type in a keyword to Yahoo! and find six web sites, but if you type in that same keyword into MSN, you may find four of the same web sites but two completely different web sites. Since different search engines can return different web sites, you may want to visit several search engines to find all the information you want off the Internet. Of course, visiting different search engines can be troublesome, so as a faster alternative, you may just want to use a meta-search engine instead.

A meta-search engine simply accesses several different search engines for you. Just type a keyword into a meta-search engine and that meta-search engine feeds that keyword into a handful of the most popular search engines. When all the search engines return their list of web sites, the meta-search engine eliminates duplicate web sites and just lists all the web sites found by all the different search engines.

Some of the more popular meta-search engines include Metacrawler (http://www.metacrawler.com), Mamma (http://www.mamma.com), Dogpile (http://www.dogpile.com), and Northern Light (http://www.northernlight.com).

Figure B-2   *The Metacrawler meta-search engine can access several search engines for you simultaneously.*

If you visit AllSearchEngines.com (http://www.allsearchengines.com), you can even find specialized search engines for specific topics such as Health & Medicine, Legal, or Travel. Such specialized search engines can often find obscure web sites that a general-purpose search engine might miss.

Download Software Drivers

If you click the Start button, click **All Programs**, and click **Windows Update**, you can keep your copy of Windows XP up to date with the latest bug fixes, security patches, and service packs. The Windows Update site can also identify the different equipment in your computer, such as video and sound cards, and load the latest drivers.

Unfortunately, the Windows Update site may not always have all the drivers you need for your various accessories such as printers, web cams, or digital cameras. In that case, you need to load the proper drivers from the CDs that came with your equipment, or just go directly to the manufacturer's web site and download the latest drivers yourself.

Since every piece of equipment in your computer needs its own driver, you need to know the exact name and model of every major component in your computer. That way, you can find the right driver for your specific printer, sound card, or video card.

AS A MATTER OF FACT *When you first turn on your computer, it often flashes the name and model of your video card on the screen. If you're fast enough, you can jot this information down so that you'll know the specific video card driver you need in case the current video driver fails for some reason.*

If the Windows Update site doesn't have the latest drivers for your components, visit the WindowsXP-Drivers.com site (http://www.windowsxp-drivers.com) to find the drivers you need (see Figure B-3). For another source for Windows XP drivers, visit ZDNet Downloads (http://downloads-zdnet.com.com).

Find Free Software

Although Windows XP includes several games, utilities, and simple business applications like WordPad and Address Book, chances are good that you'll need more software to make your computer do what you need. While you could rush out and buy a commercial program like Microsoft Office or Adobe Photoshop for several hundred dollars, you may want to consider less expensive alternatives instead.

Welcome to WindowsXP-Drivers.com

This site maintains listings of windows xp driver files available on the web, organized by company.

Home
Resources
About

	Select a Category	
BIOS / Motherboard	Digital Camera	CD-ROM / CDRW / DVD
Graphics & Video Adapter	Game Adapter	Hard Drive
IDE Controller	Input Devices (mouse, etc.)	Modem / ISDN
Monitor	Network Adapter	Notebook
Printer / Plotter / Multi-Office	Removable drive	Scanner
SCSI Adapter	Sound Card	Tape Backup

Hop to another Category

Select Category ▾
GO

Advertisement

Boost Your Connection up to 200%

Choose Your Connection

☑ 56K Dial-Up
☐ Cable
☐ DSL

Choose Your Operating System

☑ Windows 95
☐ Window 98
☐ Window 2000

? Help   ✓ OK

Figure B-3   *The WindowsXP-Drivers.com site lists different drivers by categories.*

With the growth of the Internet, many individuals and companies simply distribute their software from their web sites. So instead of going to a store to buy a boxed version of a program, you can just download a program off the Internet and install it on your computer.

Microsoft Office Alternatives

If you need a word processor and a spreadsheet, chances are good that you'll need to use Microsoft Word and Microsoft Excel. Rather than buy these two programs separately, most people just buy Microsoft Office, which includes Microsoft Word, Microsoft Excel, and Microsoft PowerPoint (a presentation program).

Unfortunately, Microsoft Office costs several hundred dollars, which could be up to half the total cost that most people paid for their computer. So rather than buy Microsoft Office, you may just want to use a free alternative called OpenOffice (http://www.openoffice.org, see Figure B-4). Like Microsoft Office, OpenOffice includes a word processor, a spreadsheet, and a presentation program. Best of all,

OpenOffice can even open and edit files originally created by Microsoft Word, Excel, or PowerPoint. That way, you can use OpenOffice and share documents with someone else who uses Microsoft Office.

Naturally, OpenOffice doesn't offer every feature of Microsoft Office, so if you need something that only Microsoft Office offers, you'll be better off buying Microsoft Office. But for most people who don't need all the fancy features loaded into Microsoft Office, OpenOffice can work just as well, and best of all, it won't cost you anything to try either.

OpenOffice may be one of the more popular free alternatives to Microsoft Office, but you may also want to consider some other free Microsoft Office alternatives that include PC602 Pro PC Suite (http://www.software602.com), EasyOffice (http://www.e-press.com), and SOT Office 2002 (http://www.sot.com/en/linux/soto). With so many free alternatives to choose from, there's a good chance that you'll find one that you like, so you won't have to buy Microsoft Office after all.

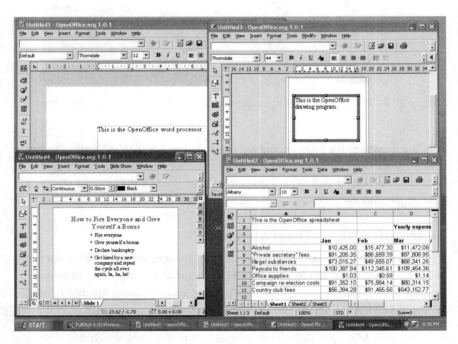

Figure B-4 *OpenOffice offers many of the same capabilities of Microsoft Office but without the cost.*

Photoshop Alternatives

With so many digital cameras on the market today, many people want a program to help them enhance any pictures they capture from their digital cameras or scanners. For professionals, there's only one choice: Adobe Photoshop.

For individuals or hobbyists, Photoshop costs several hundred dollars and is likely to be out of most people's price range. As a less expensive and simpler alternative, try the GIMP, which stands for GNU Image Manipulation Program (http://www.gimp.org).

Unlike Photoshop, the GIMP is absolutely free. While it lacks many features that Photoshop offers, the GIMP gives you basic digital editing capabilities that may be enough to either whet your appetite for the more feature-packed Photoshop or just make you realize that you aren't that interested in digitally enhancing photographs from your digital camera after all.

Shareware and Freeware Software

Believe it or not, you can find thousands of additional programs for your computer that do everything from helping you create graphical mind maps of your thoughts to helping you track expenses and income from real estate rental property. Other types of specialized programs include horse racing handicapping programs, educational children's games, lottery number tracking programs, dream interpretation programs, stock market predicting programs, and music editing software.

Some popular web sites that offer software that you can download for free include Jumbo (http://www.jumbo.com, see Figure B-5), Tucows (http://www.tucows.com), SoftDepia (http://www.softdepia.com), and Download.com (http://download. com.com).

While you can freely download as much software as you want, you'll find that many programs are either shareware, freeware, or demo versions. Shareware programs are often fully functional programs that let you try the program on your own computer so that you can decide if it's worth paying for or not. Legally, if you use a shareware program for a certain amount of time, such as thirty (30) days, you're obligated to pay for it.

Freeware programs allow you to use them at no charge whatsoever. Many freeware programs are simpler versions of a commercial program that companies throw on the Internet in the hopes that you'll like the freeware version so much that you'll be willing to pay for the full-featured commercial version of that same program.

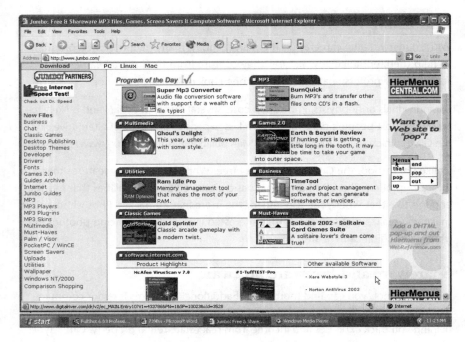

Figure B-5 *The Jumbo web site organizes software by categories.*

Demo versions are usually crippled versions of the complete program. This gives you a chance to use the program for as long as you want, although you won't be able to do anything really important with it such as print or save any files. The idea behind a demo program is to encourage you to experiment with the demo and get you to pay for the full-featured commercial version eventually.

> **AS A MATTER OF FACT** *Before you download any files off the Internet, make sure you have the latest version of an anti-virus program to scan your files first.*

By downloading software off the Internet, you can find a variety of low-cost or free programs that can make your computer do exactly what you want. Now you just have to figure out what you want your computer to do after all.

Account   A way to divide and limit access to one person to use a computer. For security, an account can be protected with a password. See also *Password.*

Address   A unique name that identifies a web site. Common web site addresses include www.yahoo.com and www.whitehouse.gov.

ALT key   A special key on the keyboard that modifies the function of other keys. The **ALT** key is rarely pressed by itself. Instead, it is often pressed with another key such as **ALT+F4**, which means to hold down the **ALT** key, press the **F4** key, and then release both keys at the same time.

AOL   An acronym for America Online. AOL is a popular Internet service provider that allows access to the Internet for a fee.

Back button   A button that lets you view the preceding contents of a window, such as in a browser or in a Help system of a program. See also *Forward button.*

Broadband access   A fast connection to the Internet, usually through a dedicated line provided by a telephone or cable television company. See also *Dial-up access.*

Browser   A type of program designed to view web pages stored on the World Wide Web. See also *Internet Explorer.*

Bug   A problem or flaw in a program. Bugs can be as mildly annoying as displaying weird images on the screen or extremely serious to the point of keeping a program from working at all. When Microsoft discovers another bug in Windows XP, the company may release a patch or service pack to fix it. See also *Patch* and *Service pack.*

Button A rectangular part of the screen that displays the name of a command you can choose. To choose that command, you can click that button.

Cascade To display multiple windows, one slightly behind the other like cards in a stack. See also *Tile*.

CD+RW A type of compact disc that can be rewritten over and over again. To write to a CD+RW disc, you must have a CD+RW drive.

CD-R A type of compact disc that can be written to just once. To write to a CD-R disc, you must have a rewritable CD drive.

Check box An empty square that appears next to an option. To select that option, click in the empty square so that a check mark appears inside.

Click To point at something, press the left mouse button, and then release the left mouse button. Clicking is often a way to give commands to your computer. See also *Right-click*.

Clips Parts of a video file. To edit a video, you arrange clips and edit the start and end of each clip. See also *Windows Movie Maker*.

Close box A red box with an X in it that lets you close a window and shut down the program in that window.

Compact Flash A portable storage device used with many digital cameras and handheld computers. See also *Multimedia Card, SmartMedia,* and *Memory Stick*.

Control Panel A window that displays commands that let you change different parts of Windows XP. Whenever you want to change the way Windows XP works, you can do it through the Control Panel.

Copy To temporarily store a selected item in memory. After you copy an item, the next step is to move the mouse pointer or cursor to tell Windows XP where to put that copied item by using the Paste command. The shortcut keystroke to choose the Copy command is **CTRL+C**. See also *Cut* and *Paste*.

Crash When a program or the entire computer no longer responds to any commands and cannot be controlled in any way. See also *Reboot*.

CTRL key A special key on the keyboard that modifies the function of other keys. The **CTRL** key is rarely pressed by itself. Instead, it is usually pressed with another key such as **CTRL+S**, which means to hold down the **CTRL** key, press the **S** key, and then release both keys at the same time.

Cursor A blinking vertical line that tells you where text will appear if you type something.

Cursor key A set of four keys that point up, down, right, and left, which let you move the cursor on the screen. Also called the arrow keys.

Cut To remove a selected item and store it in memory. After you cut an item, the next step is to move the mouse pointer or cursor to tell Windows XP where you want to put that cut item by using the Paste command. The combination of the Cut and Paste commands lets you move an item to another location. The shortcut keystroke to choose the Cut command is **CTRL+X**. See also *Copy* and *Paste*.

Data Information that you or the computer creates and saves for future use. Computers store data in files. See also *File*.

Database A program designed for storing organized chunks of information such as names and addresses or serial numbers and item names. Two popular database programs for Windows XP are Microsoft Access and FileMaker Pro.

Desktop The screen that Windows XP displays when there are no programs running. The desktop consists of wallpaper, icons, and the taskbar.

Dial-up access A connection to the Internet through an ordinary telephone line. See also *Broadband access*.

Dialog box A box that lets you give additional information to the computer to perform a specific command, such as when the computer wants to know how many pages to print of a file.

Digital camera A special camera that stores images on a removable device, such as a floppy disk, a Compact Flash card, or a Memory Stick. Digital cameras can often connect to a computer so that you can transfer images directly from the camera to your computer. See also *Compact Flash, Multimedia Card, SmartMedia,* and *Memory Stick*.

Digital image A still image captured by a digital recording device such as a camera or camcorder.

Digital video A series of moving images that can be edited like videotape but that offers higher resolution and quality, like conventional film. See also *Windows Movie Maker*.

Disk Cleanup A program that comes with Windows XP, which can automatically remove unnecessary files, thereby reducing the space used up on your hard disk.

Disk Defragmenter   A program that comes with Windows XP, which lets you reorganize the files stored on your hard disk to make your computer run faster.

Double-click   To click the left mouse button twice rapidly. See also *Click* and *Right-click*. This is usually done to open or run the selected file or program.

Drag   To hold down the left mouse button and move the mouse. Dragging is often used to select multiple items or move a single item on the screen.

Driver   A special program designed to tell Windows XP how to use a certain piece of equipment such as a printer or a scanner.

DSL   An acronym for digital subscriber line, meaning a special telephone line that allows broadband access to the Internet.

DVD   An acronym for Digital Video Disc. A DVD stores video images such as feature-length movies.

E-mail   A system for sending messages over the Internet.

Encryption   A method for scrambling data so that it can be unscrambled only with a specific password.

ESC key   A special key on the keyboard that often lets you close a menu or get rid of a dialog box by pressing it. The **ESC** key usually appears in the upper-left corner of most keyboards.

File   A collection of related information stored on a disk, such as a hard disk or a floppy disk. A file can contain a word processor document, a list of names and addresses in a database, or a video.

File attachment   The part of an e-mail message that includes a file. File attachments can be handy for sending word processor documents or programs by e-mail.

File format   A specific way to store data. Every program stores data in a specific way that other programs may not be able to understand.

Firewall   A special program that can limit access to your computer through the Internet. Often used to protect a computer against malicious computer users.

FireWire   A special connection used to transfer digital video from a digital camcorder to your computer. Not all computers have a FireWire port. Also referred to as an IEEE 1394 port or an iLink port on Sony computers.

Folder A way to divide a disk into compartments. A folder can contain both files and other folders. To view the contents of a folder, you need to use the Windows Explorer program. See also *Windows Explorer.*

Forward button A button that lets you view the next contents of a window, such as in a browser or in a Help system of a program. The Forward button often appears dimmed until you use the Back button first. See also *Back button.*

Function key A special key on the keyboard that can give a command to your computer. Most keyboards include twelve function keys labeled **F1** through **F12**, along with additional function keys such as the Windows Logo key or the **INSERT** or **DELETE** keys.

Gigabyte A unit of measurement that defines how much data a device can store, such as a hard disk. One gigabyte equals 1,024 million bytes, or 1.024 billion bytes. See also *Megabyte.*

Hacker A person who understands and can manipulate computers. Malicious hackers often break into computers to destroy or modify data.

Hard drive A magnetic disk that lets you store and erase data. The size of hard drives is often measured in gigabytes (GB). See also *Gigabyte.*

Hardware Any device that you can touch, which connects to your computer.

Help system A collection of instructions and troubleshooting tips that comes with every program. To access a program's help system, press **F1**.

Home button The button that displays the home page. In Internet Explorer, your home page is the first web site you see when you connect to the Internet. In a Help system, the home page is the first screen that appears in the Help window every time you load the Help system.

Home page The first screen that appears when you load a browser or the Help system of a program.

Hyperlink A text or graphic on a web page that you can click to go to another web page or web site.

Icon A miniature picture that represents a program or file. Icons appear on the desktop and in dialog boxes such as the Open dialog box. An icon often appears with a name displayed underneath or to one side.

Install The process of copying a program to your computer. See also *Uninstall.*

Internet The worldwide connection of computers that share information such as e-mail or web pages with one another.

Internet Explorer A program that comes with Windows XP, which lets you view web pages stored on the World Wide Web.

ISP An acronym for Internet service provider, meaning any company that allows access to the Internet. See also *Dial-up access* and *Broadband access*.

Keyboard A device for typing in characters and giving commands to the computer. See also *Mouse*.

LAN An acronym for local area network. A LAN connects multiple computers together so that they can share files and equipment such as printers or modems.

LCD An acronym for liquid crystal display. LCDs are often found in flat-screen monitors, laptop computers, and handheld computers.

List box A box that displays a downward-pointing arrow that you can click to see more choices.

Maximize To expand a window to cover the entire screen. See also *Minimize*.

Megabyte A unit of measurement that defines how much data a device can store, such as your computer's memory. One megabyte equals 1,048,576 bytes, where one byte can store one character, such as a letter or a number. See also *Gigabyte*.

Memory Temporary storage that a computer uses to run programs and store data. Memory is often measured in megabytes or gigabytes. Before you turn off your computer, you should copy all data from memory to a disk such as a hard disk or a compact disc.

Memory Stick A portable storage device, developed by Sony for use in many digital cameras and handheld computers. See also *Compact Flash, Multimedia Card,* and *SmartMedia*.

Menu, pop-up A list of commands that pops up in the middle of the screen, usually when you right-click an item. See also *Right-click*.

Menu, pull-down A list of commands that appears at the top of a window. Pull-down menus list every possible command available in a program.

Minimize To shrink a window to a small button that appears on the taskbar. See also *Maximize*.

Modem   A device that lets your computer communicate over a telephone or cable television line to access the Internet.

Modifier keys   Special keys that you press with another key to give a command to the computer. Common modifier keys include the **ALT**, **CTRL**, and **SHIFT** keys. See also **ALT** *key* and **CTRL** *key.*

Mouse   A pointing device that you slide on a flat surface to move a pointer on the screen. See also *Trackball* and *Touchpad.*

Mouse pointer   An icon, commonly an arrow, that lets you point at different parts of the screen using a pointing device such as a mouse, a trackball, or a touchpad. The mouse pointer often changes appearance depending on what you may be doing.

Mouse wheel   A third button that appears as a rubber wheel in the middle of the mouse. Spinning the mouse wheel scrolls a page up or down. Pressing the mouse wheel and then moving the mouse lets you scroll up or down faster.

MSN   An acronym for Microsoft Network. MSN is both an Internet service provider and a web site (www.msn.com).

Multimedia Card   A portable storage device for use in many digital cameras. See also *Compact Flash, SmartMedia,* and *Memory Stick.*

Network   A group of two or more computers that can share files, programs, or equipment such as a printer.

Operating system   A special program that controls your computer and provides commands that let you tell your computer what to do. Windows XP is just one of many operating systems available.

Outlook Express   A program that comes with Windows XP, which lets you send and receive e-mail. See also *E-mail.*

Pane   Part of a window that's divided in two or more sections. Panes allow a window to display different information at the same time.

Parallel port   A connection in the back of the computer that lets you plug additional hardware to the computer. Most devices use USB ports rather than parallel ports nowadays. See also *USB.*

Password   A secret word or phrase that gives you access to an account on a computer. See also *Account.*

Paste   To place a previously copied or cut item. The Paste command is used only after you have already used the Cut or Copy command. The shortcut keystroke to choose the Paste command is **CTRL+V**. See also *Cut* and *Copy*.

Patch   A file that fixes one or more problems in a program. See also *Windows Update*.

PDA   An acronym for personal digital assistant. A PDA is a handheld computer that enables you to store data and copy it to your desktop or laptop computer.

Pentium   A name trademarked by Intel to define a family of microprocessor chips used to run many computers that use Windows XP.

Pixel   A single point of light used to display images on the screen. The collection of multiple pixels on the screen determines how sharp or blurry an image appears. See also *Resolution*.

Playlist   A collection of one or more audio files that you can listen to through the Windows Media Player. See also *Windows Media Player*.

Plug and Play   A term used to describe hardware that you can plug into your computer and it works—in theory. Often mocked by the similar term, Plug and Pray, which more accurately reflects the frustration you may encounter when trying to get different hardware to work with your computer.

Power Toys   A collection of unsupported programs from Microsoft designed to enhance the way Windows XP works.

Quick Launch toolbar   A list of icons that appears next to the Start button on the taskbar and gives you fast access to your favorite programs.

Radio button   An empty circle that appears next to an option. To select that option, click in the empty circle so that a black dot appears inside. Radio buttons appear in groups of two or more; you can choose only one radio button in a group.

RAM   An acronym for random access memory. See also *Memory*.

Reboot   The process of shutting down a computer and starting it back up again. Sometimes a reboot is the only way to recover from a computer crash. See also *Crash*.

Recycle Bin   A special folder that stores deleted items so that you can recover them at a later time. If you want to permanently delete an item, you have to empty it from the Recycle Bin.

Removable drive   A device that can store data and be moved from one computer to another. The most common removable drives are the floppy disk and the compact disc.

Resolution   The number of pixels used to display an image. Common resolutions for your screen include 800 × 600 and 1024 × 768. See also *Pixel*.

Restore down   To change a window from covering the entire screen (maximized) to covering only part of the screen. The Restore down button is available only in a window that has already been maximized. See also *Maximize*.

Restore point   A point of time in the past that preserves your settings for Windows XP. A restore point is used by the System Restore command to return your computer to a previous configuration when everything actually worked. See also *Crash*.

Right-click   While pointing at something on the screen, to press and then release the right mouse button. Right-clicking is a way to display a menu of commands. See also *Click*.

Scanner   A device that can capture pictures of printed material and store it on a computer.

Screensaver   A program that runs after you don't use your computer for a certain amount of time, such as three minutes. Screensavers display ever-changing images.

Scroll bars   Vertical and horizontal slides that appear on the bottom and right side of a window and let you slide the contents of a window up and down or right and left.

Search engine   A special web site that lets you search for other web sites on the World Wide Web. Two common search engines are MSN and Yahoo!

Serial port   A connection on the back of the computer that lets you plug additional hardware to the computer. Most devices use USB ports rather than serial ports nowadays. See also *USB*.

Service pack   A collection of updates and bug fixes stored in a single file that you can use to update your copy of Windows XP.

Skin   The appearance of the Windows Media Player. To change the appearance of the Windows Media Player, you can choose from one of many skins.

Slider   A way to give information to a computer by dragging the mouse right and left or up and down. The position of the slider gives a fixed value to the computer.

SmartMedia   A portable storage device for use in many digital cameras. See also *Compact Flash, Multimedia Card,* and *Memory Stick.*

Software   Any program that makes your computer do something.

Spreadsheet   A program designed to graph numbers and make calculations quick and easy. The most popular spreadsheet for Windows XP is Microsoft Excel.

Start button   A green button that appears on the taskbar, which allows you access to all the programs stored on your computer.

Tab   (1) A key that moves the cursor a fixed amount of spaces, often used in word processors to indent a paragraph. (2) Part of a dialog box that lets you access multiple options.

Task Manager   A program that lets you see which programs are currently running, switch to another program, or shut a program down. The Task Manager can be especially useful to shut down an unresponsive program.

Taskbar   A thin strip that appears on your screen (usually the bottom) that displays the Start button and icons of any currently running programs. See also *Start button.*

Text box   A box that lets you type information into the computer.

Tile   To display multiple windows side by side or stacked on top of each other. See also *Cascade.*

Timeline   A collection of clips that shows the order that you want to play the clips in a video. See also *Windows Movie Maker.*

Title bar   The top border of a window or dialog box that often displays the title of the window or dialog box and displays the Minimize and Maximize/Restore Down buttons and the close box. If you drag the title bar, you can move a window or dialog box.

Toolbar   A collection of icons that usually appear near the top of a window. Each icon represents a commonly used command, so toolbars offer a shortcut alternative to using pull-down menus. See also *Menu, pull-down.*

Touchpad   A pointing device commonly found on laptop computers, which lets you slide your finger across a surface to move the mouse pointer on the screen. See also *Mouse.*

Trackball   A pointing device that remains stationary but has a ball that you can spin to control the mouse pointer on the screen. Trackballs are common alternatives to a mouse. See also *Mouse.*

Uninstall   The process of removing a program from your computer. See also *Install.*

USB   An acronym for Universal Serial Bus, meaning a special port that allows a variety of devices to plug in to your computer, such as a printer, a scanner, or a digital camera.

Virus   A program that attaches itself to files and can destroy data. The safest way to stop viruses is with an anti-virus program.

Wallpaper   An image that appears on the desktop to add color and variety to your screen. See also *Desktop.*

Webcam   A special camera that broadcasts live video images from your computer.

Web page   A single screen that displays text and graphics that computers all over the world can view through the Internet.

Web site   A collection of one or more web pages. See also *Address.*

Window   A box that displays the contents of a program. A window can cover all or part of the screen.

Windows 2000, Windows Me, Windows 98, Windows 95   Previous versions of Microsoft Windows.

Windows Explorer   A program that lets you manage files and folders on your computer. See also *File* and *Folder.*

Windows Media Player   A program that comes with Windows XP, which lets you play audio and video files.

Windows Movie Maker   A program that comes with Windows XP, which allows you to edit digital video movies.

Windows Update   A command found on the All Programs menu that allows you to download the latest updates for Windows XP.

Windows XP Home Edition   The version of Windows XP designed for home and small business use.

Windows XP Professional Edition   The version of Windows XP designed for large business and corporate use.

Wizard   A special type of dialog box that guides you through a specific task, step-by-step, such as installing a printer.

Word processor   A program designed to help you write, format, and print text. The most popular word processor for Windows XP is Microsoft Word.

World Wide Web   The collection of web sites all over the world, connected by the Internet.

Index

References to figures are in italics.

D

E

graphic links. *See* links

grouping programs on the
taskbar, 33

H

hackers, 183

hard drive
cleaning, 148–149
defined, 183
defragmenting, 149–150
reorganizing, 149–150
restoring, 150–152

hardware
adding, 112–113
defined, 183

help
browsing, 16–17
clicking, 13–15
defined, 183
Help Index, 16–17
Help window, 13–17
searching, 15–16

hibernation mode, 39

hiding
icons, 31
taskbar, 32

highlighting data, 5

History list, 74–76

Home button, 183

HOME key, 8

home page, 77–78
defined, 183

hyperlinks
defined, 183
See also links

I

icons, 9, 53
adding, 29–30
Auto Arrange command, 31
customizing, 27–31
defined, 183
deleting, 27–29
desktop, 96–97, 102–103
dragging, 98
hiding, 31
loading documents using,
102–103
moving, 30
paper clip, 84–85
pinning, 98
rearranging, 30–31
renaming, 30
unused, 28–29
See also views

installing
from a CD, 94
defined, 183
drivers, 112–113
from the Internet, 94–95
Power Toys, 164
See also uninstalling

Internet
browsing, 69–78
defined, 184
installing programs from the,
94–95
preparing to connect to, 68–69

Internet Explorer, 69
Address list box, 74
Back button, 72–73
defined, 184

INTERNATIONAL CONTACT INFORMATION

AUSTRALIA
McGraw-Hill Book Company Australia Pty. Ltd.
TEL +61-2-9900-1800
FAX +61-2-9878-8881
http://www.mcgraw-hill.com.au
books-it_sydney@mcgraw-hill.com

CANADA
McGraw-Hill Ryerson Ltd.
TEL +905-430-5000
FAX +905-430-5020
http://www.mcgraw-hill.ca

GREECE, MIDDLE EAST, & AFRICA
(Excluding South Africa)
McGraw-Hill Hellas
TEL +30-210-6560-990
TEL +30-210-6560-993
TEL +30-210-6560-994
FAX +30-210-6545-525

MEXICO (Also serving Latin America)
McGraw-Hill Interamericana Editores S.A. de C.V.
TEL +525-117-1583
FAX +525-117-1589
http://www.mcgraw-hill.com.mx
fernando_castellanos@mcgraw-hill.com

SINGAPORE (Serving Asia)
McGraw-Hill Book Company
TEL +65-863-1580
FAX +65-862-3354
http://www.mcgraw-hill.com.sg
mghasia@mcgraw-hill.com

SOUTH AFRICA
McGraw-Hill South Africa
TEL +27-11-622-7512
FAX +27-11-622-9045
robyn_swanepoel@mcgraw-hill.com

SPAIN
McGraw-Hill/Interamericana de España, S.A.U.
TEL +34-91-180-3000
FAX +34-91-372-8513
http://www.mcgraw-hill.es
professional@mcgraw-hill.es

UNITED KINGDOM, NORTHERN,
EASTERN, & CENTRAL EUROPE
McGraw-Hill Education Europe
TEL +44-1-628-502500
FAX +44-1-628-770224
http://www.mcgraw-hill.co.uk
computing_neurope@mcgraw-hill.com

ALL OTHER INQUIRIES Contact:
Osborne/McGraw-Hill
TEL +1-510-549-6600
FAX +1-510-883-7600
http://www.osborne.com
omg_international@mcgraw-hill.com

Finally!

because technology should improve your life, not complicate it...

The No Nonsense approach at a no frills price.